2011

IT Architecture – Essential Practice for IT Business Solutions

Peter Beijer

Enterprise Architect, Hewlett-Packard Nederland B.V.

Theo de Klerk

Solution Architect, Hewlett-Packard Nederland B.V.

Copyright © 2010 Peter Beijer and Theo de Klerk

All rights reserved. No part of this publication may be reproduced, stored in a database or retrieval system or transmitted in any form or by any means, electronic, mechanical, photocopying, recording or otherwise, without the prior written permission of the copyright holders.

While every effort has been made to ensure the reliability of the information presented in this publication, the copyright holders neither guarantee the accuracy of the data contained herein nor accept responsibility for errors or omissions, or their consequences.

First published in 2010 by Lulu.com

ISBN 978-1-4457-0603-0

Conceived and designed: Peter Beijer and Theo de Klerk

Editorial and Graphics Consultant: Kristin Rounds

Printed by Lulu.com (www.lulu.com)

Order number: 8401663

Contents

FOREWORD XIII

PREFACE XV

1. **WHAT IS IT ARCHITECTURE?** 1
   ARCHITECTURE AS ESSENTIALS 4
   HOW ARCHITECTURE DIFFERS FROM DESIGN 6
   CONCLUSION 8

2. **APPLICABILITY OF IT ARCHITECTURE** 11
   WHEN TO APPLY ARCHITECTURE? 12
   WHERE TO APPLY ARCHITECTURE? 13
   BUSINESS 13
   INFORMATION 15
   APPLICATIONS 16
   INFRASTRUCTURE 16
   SOLUTIONS 17
   THE ENTERPRISE CONTEXT 18
   TYING IT TOGETHER 20
   CONCLUSION 21

3. **THE VALUE OF IT ARCHITECTURE** 23
   ABOUT VALUE 24
   VALUE TO SPONSORS 25
   VALUE TO USERS 26
   VALUE TO PRACTITIONERS 26
   CONCLUSION 27

4. **OVERVIEW OF HPGM FOR ITSA** 29
   THE ARCHITECTURE FRAMEWORK 30
   THE ITSA FRAMEWORK 32
   THE ARCHITECTURE CONCEPT METHODOLOGY 32
   THE ARCHITECTURE BLUEPRINT METHODOLOGY 32
   OTHER FRAMEWORKS AND METHODOLOGIES 33
   CONCLUSION 33

5. **BUSINESS DRIVERS AND GOALS** 35
   BUSINESS DRIVERS 36
   BUSINESS GOALS 38
   BUSINESS METRICS 40
   CONCLUSION 43

6. STAKEHOLDERS AND VIEWS 45

STAKEHOLDERS 46
VIEWS IN ITSA 49
THE FOUR VIEWS REVISITED 51
THE FOCUS OF VIEWS 54
VIEW DEPENDENCIES ON BUSINESS TYPE 55
CONCLUSION 57

7. ARCHITECTURAL PRINCIPLES 59

THE PURPOSE OF PRINCIPLES 60
RANGE AND REACH OF PRINCIPLES 61
THE POWER OF PRINCIPLES 63
PRINCIPLES IN ITSA 64
THE WORLD OF PRINCIPLES 70
PRINCIPLES DIFFER FROM GOALS 72
PRINCIPLES DIFFER FROM REQUIREMENTS 73
PRINCIPLES DIFFER FROM POLICIES 74
CONCLUSION 75

8. EFFECTIVE PRINCIPLES 77

PRINCIPLE STATEMENT: CONTENT 78
PRINCIPLE INDEPENDENCE: ORTHOGONALITY 80
PRINCIPLE GUIDANCE: AUTHORITY 82
PRINCIPLE LINKING: RATIONALE 83
IMPLICATIONS: CONDITIONS ON PRINCIPLE-DESCRIBED STATE 84
OBSTACLES: ISSUES ON THE PRINCIPLE BEYOND OUR CONTROL 84
CONCLUSION 85

9. TOPIC AREAS 87

FOCUS ON ESSENTIALS: TOPIC AREAS 88
HOW TO IDENTIFY SUITABLE TOPIC AREAS 89
CHARACTERISTICS OF TOPIC AREAS 92
EXAMPLE TOPIC AREAS 92
CONCLUSION 94

10. ARCHITECTURAL MODELS 95

WHAT IS A MODEL? 96
WHEN TO USE MODELS? 97
REQUIREMENTS FOR ARCHITECTURAL MODELS 98
MODELS IN ITSA 101
A STANDARD FOR MODELS 102
MODELS BY ITSA VIEW 102
CONCLUSION 103

11. ARCHITECTURAL STANDARDS 105
- The Purpose of Standards 105
- Standards in ITSA 106
- Standards versus Requirements 107
- Conclusion 108

12. ARCHITECTURAL REQUIREMENTS 109
- Why Architectural Requirements and What Are They? 110
- Then What Are Project Requirements? 112
- What Do Architectural Requirements Look Like? 112
- How Do Requirements Differ from Principles? 113
- How Requirements Relate to Principles 114
- A Simple Example 115
- How Others Treat Requirements 116
- Conclusion 117

13. PUTTING EVERYTHING TOGETHER 119
- Bridging the Gap 120
- Traversing the Gap 123
- Architecture Blueprint Deliverables 124
- Governance of IT Architecture and IT 128
- Prepare for the Future and Use the Past 131
- Conclusion 133

14. ARCHITECTURE AND PROJECT MANAGEMENT 135
- The Role of Project Management 136
- Architecture from a Project Management View 137
- An Integral Approach 139
- Conclusion 141

15. THE IT ARCHITECT PROFESSION 143
- Vitruvius 144
- What Characterizes the Profession of IT Architect? 146
- Am I Doing Design or Architecture? 147
- The Architect Career Path 149
- Certification 151
- Conclusion 153

16. RESOURCES FOR IT ARCHITECTURE 155
- Links 155
- Books 156
- Journals 157
- Communities and Institutes 157

APPENDIX A – SWOT ANALYSIS FOR DRIVERS AND GOALS 159
  The SWOT Focus Areas – Where Are We? 159
  The SWOT to Identify Business Drivers and Goals 161

APPENDIX B – THE BALANCED SCORE CARD FOR TOPIC AREAS 165
  The Balanced Score Card 165
  The BSC and topic areas 168
  BSC and Product Selection 169

APPENDIX C – SAMPLE PRINCIPLE STATEMENTS 173
  Organizations with No Core-IT Business 173
  Organizations with Core-IT Business 175

APPENDIX D – TOOL BAG 179
  Principles Capture Template 179
  Requirements Capture Template 184
  Model Capture Template 186

APPENDIX E – CASE STUDY: INFORMATION WORKER 2.0 189
  The Case 190
  Business Drivers and Goals 190
  Topic Areas 191
  Business View 193
  Functional View 195
  Technical View 197
  Implementation View 199

APPENDIX F – HPGM FOR ITSA, THE JOURNEY 201

ABOUT THE AUTHORS 213

INDEX 215

Figures

Figure 1: Complexity and newness as a measure for architecture need..........12
Figure 2: Areas of interest for architecture in the enterprise............................14
Figure 3: Models as devices for understanding...15
Figure 4: Hierarchies of areas of interest for architecture in the enterprise...19
Figure 5: Architecture in various domains within the enterprise....................20
Figure 6: The four views with architectural elements......................................31
Figure 7: The ITSA framework as foundation for methodologies.................32
Figure 8: Business drivers, goals and choices...39
Figure 9: Business goals drive the architecture..42
Figure 10: Stakeholder types..47
Figure 11: Power-interest grid..48
Figure 12: Stakeholders and views...50
Figure 13: Views and their main concerns 52
Figure 14: Narrowing down of solution choices...54
Figure 15: Circular influence among views..55
Figure 16 Topics in IT centric and non-IT centric organizations 57
Figure 17: The solution and its principles in the architecture space...............62
Figure 18: Principles in the ITSA framework...64
Figure 19: Link between principles of views..67
Figure 20: ITSA goal-means hierarchy of principles 70
Figure 21: Coherent requirements result from architecture 74
Figure 22: Spectrum for various principle topics 78
Figure 23: Principles must not decompose into composite principles...........81
Figure 24: Individual principles that sum up must be combined 81
Figure 25: Independent principles by removing commonalities.....................82
Figure 26: Topic areas in different views..89
Figure 27: From initial problem statement to topic areas.................................91
Figure 28: Models and their levels of abstraction...100
Figure 29: Models link to principles and other models..................................101

Figure 30: Standards in the ITSA framework 107
Figure 31: The V-lifecycle.. 111
Figure 32: Relationships of requirements 114
Figure 33: Principle(s) motivate requirement(s)... 115
Figure 34: Bridging business and IT through architecture.............................. 121
Figure 35: The big picture from initial architecture to solution project........ 124
Figure 36: IT governance and architecture governance 130
Figure 37: Reuse and actual use... 132
Figure 38: Extracting architectural elements for reuse 133
Figure 39: Relation architect, project manager, and business sponsor.......... 141
Figure 40: Cascading architectures 147
Figure 41: SWOT analysis chart.. 159
Figure 42: SWOT as a start to elicit raw business drivers and goals 163
Figure 43: Balanced Score Card.. 166
Figure 44: Balanced Score Card provides topic areas 169
Figure 45: Strength/Weakness analysis 190
Figure 46: Topic areas applied in each view.. 191
Figure 47: Type of workers 194
Figure 48: Types of workplace functionality for worker types...................... 196
Figure 49: Information Worker 2.0 technical model...................................... 198

Tables

Table 1: The concept of architecture versus design 8
Table 2: The four architecture views 30
Table 3: Views and their typical stakeholders 51
Table 4: The structure of a principle 65
Table 5: Example action structure 70
Table 6: Example principles in the spectrum of various domains 79
Table 7: Possible linkages of rationales 83
Table 8: Documenting models 102
Table 9: Architectural requirement structure 112
Table 10: Principles versus requirements 114
Table 11: Architecture versus project management 140
Table 12: Perspectives on architect competences 145
Table 13: The architect versus the designer 149
Table 14: SWOT quadrant combinations 162
Table 15 Balanced Score Card to elicit topic areas 170

The American composer Alan Hovhaness (1911 – 2000) speaks of his music in almost metaphysical terms, very comparable to the essence of IT architecture: 'The reason I like Oriental music is that everything has a firm center. All music with a center is tonal. Music without a center is fine for a minute or two, but it soon sounds all the same . . . Things which are very complicated tend to disappear and get lost. Simplicity is difficult, not easy. Beauty is simple. All unnecessary elements are removed – only essence remains.'

Foreword

I first encountered HP Global Method for IT Strategy and Architecture (HPGM for ITSA) as CSAM (Compaq Services Architecture Methodology) in August 2000. I had been 'doing architecture' in one form or another for the prior fifteen years, but whatever methodological discipline I brought to bear on my practice was an ad hoc assembly of approaches borrowed mostly from software engineering and general systems thinking. CSAM was a revelation; it codified, in a retrospectively obvious way, what I had been trying to do by the seat of my pants. For the subsequent seven years, first as a member and later as the lead of the worldwide Architecture Profession Office for HP Services I had the opportunity to use, teach and further develop CSAM and then HPGM for ITSA. During that time my esteem and respect for ITSA has only grown.

Now, as VP, Skills and Capabilities for The Open Group, I frequently sit on review boards for The Open Group's IT Architect Certification (ITAC) program, and review submissions of IT architectural methods for approval as ITAC recognized methods. As such, I have seen a lot about how IT architecture is practiced and the methods IT architects use. Most of these methods are project management lifecycle models for architecture projects; they say what things you should do or produce in what order, but they generally say little about how to do or produce these things. Only a few of these methods are heuristics for producing architectural work products; ITSA is one of these few.

Virtually all of these methods are proprietary, and the publication of this book is therefore a significant milestone in the professionalization of the discipline of IT architecture. Hewlett-Packard deserves considerable credit for sharing this powerfully effective method with the IT architecture community at large.

It was through CSAM and ITSA that I first met and got to know and respect Peter and Theo, and I am pleased that our collegial relationship has become an enduring friendship, despite our being separated by the Atlantic Ocean. This book has long been a gleam in the collective eye of the HP Services architecture community and I am especially pleased that it is Peter and Theo who have brought that vision to fruition.

Leonard (Len) Fehskens

VP, Skills and Capabilities for The Open Group

Preface

> *There is nothing more difficult to take in hand, more perilous to conduct or more uncertain in its success than to take the lead in the introduction of a new order of things.*
>
> ~Machiavelli

When writing a book it is difficult to decide what must be included and what must be left out and what needs to be the level of detail for each topic. Certainly with IT architecture – simply called *architecture* in the remaining text for short – this is a challenge, as this relatively young discipline is gaining so much attention lately and on occasion results in lively discussions on the subject. Part of that discussion is very existential: what is architecture, and what makes architecture an architecture? Often this discussion also covers and even mixes the relations that architecture has with other disciplines like project management, design, and requirements engineering. Also, the distinct difference between architecture and design or engineering gives rise to the frequent question: where does architecture end and design begin?

The architecture discipline is maturing and we see many good developments demonstrated in the field on architecture frameworks, methodologies, and the art of practicing architecture. These include the idea of certification in the field of architecture; not only on methodologies, but more importantly also on the behavior and skills of practitioners in which experience in *doing* IT architecture is paramount. These are welcome developments that lead to a better profession, and presumably to better application of information technology to solve business problems. Despite the current level of maturity the architecture discipline has reached today, there still is a lack of understanding of what IT architecture actually constitutes, what potential it has, and how it should be practiced..

Hewlett-Packard (HP), with its acquired companies Digital Equipment Corporation and Compaq Computer Corporation, has a long history with IT architecture since it adapted the first insights and experiences from the PRISM research project,[1] which studied ways to implement information systems back in the late 1980s. This book is about practicing IT architecture,

---

[1] Partnership for Research in Information Systems Management (PRISM), a management research service of CSC Index, Inc. and Hammer and Company, Inc. in 1986.

set against the background of the practical insights gained at HP and formalized in the HP methodology for IT Strategy and Architecture (ITSA).

Architecture today is quite an overloaded term, meaning different things to different people. Too many practitioners think of architecture as a project management lifecycle model that calls for the creation of architectural artifacts, instead of the *heuristics* for the creation of those artifacts. As a result, most writing about IT architecture today focuses on the various frameworks in the market and glosses over the question of what architecture is really about. It fails to distinguish architecture in a meaningful way from high level design. This focus leads IT architects to concentrate on the content of architecture frameworks instead of on the real concerns sponsors face. In other words, IT architects fail to claim their true role in the business-IT relationship, a role that is both existential and meaningful to the business. Therefore, we must return to the essence presented by the following questions: a) what defines architecture as architecture, and b) what characterizes a practitioner in this field – the IT architect?

Let us return to the consideration of what scope and level of detail we consider appropriate to explore the issues raised here. If we want to avoid glossing over things, there is only one way to it. We must be very specific and discuss the issues using a methodology that is complete and exhaustive. This implies the exclusion of open architecture frameworks, as they are incomplete by nature. One such publicly available open framework is TOGAF (The Open Group Architecture Framework). To address the issues and to make this a practical book, we need to draw on an architecture methodology that provides the practical level of detail, and of which the authors are authorities and have intimate knowledge. For this reason, we have deliberately restricted ourselves to the methodology we know best and have applied for many years: HP Global Method for IT Strategy and Architecture (HPGM for ITSA, or ITSA for short). The reader will not find discussions and coverage of other, often proprietary, methodologies that exist in the market. However, our choice to use ITSA should not constrain the reader, as it is possible to apply the practices presented in this book to other architecture practices, frameworks, and methodologies.

These thoughts motivated us to give the reader the reasons and, above all, the understanding of when IT architecture is needed, what it must contain in general, and why HP does it in this particular way with its ITSA approach. We want to give the reader insight into the architecture methodology HP employs as a core competence in defining its IT solutions – doing architecture to solve problems or exploit opportunities, and not doing architecture simply for the sake of architecture. The attentive reader will appreciate the beauty of the seamless chain of justification that ITSA deploys to solve a problem in an unprecedented way. It puts the architect in the position to challenge both business *and* IT, and to invent innovative solutions that explore unknown ground. This is where true architecture has immense added value and differentiates itself from design or engineering.

Writing about the discipline of IT architecture makes it mandatory for us to include aspects of the IT architecture profession. The two go hand in hand, and this is a reason to discuss what constitutes the IT architect profession and how it differs so distinctively from any other IT profession, but also its collaborative relationship with these professions. The content of the book quite naturally falls into three parts:

- Chapters 1 through 3 discuss the concept of IT architecture, its origin, its application and what it brings for the business, IT users, and practioners.

- Chapters 4 through 12 provide a detailed explanation of the mechanics, framework, and methodology of the HP architecture approach (ITSA).

- Chapters 13 through 16 show how everything ties together and is used in practice in projects, IT governance, and how architect and project manager play a collaborative role in architectural endeavors.

As practicing architects, we both have come a long way in applying IT architecture the way we do it now. We learned from our mistakes, discovering things the hard way. We were lucky to be part of a community that shared its insight and experiences and made our journey a joint learning exercise.

We are indebted to all our fellow travelers who made it possible for us to write this book. Several people played important roles in the preparation of this book: Rob Kruijk, one of the founding fathers of ITSA, on how architecture developed from the PRISM results into an architecture method now pivotal within HP; Leonard Fehskens on ferreting out essential truths about IT architecture; Roberto Rivera, who provided 'archeological' research on IT architecture; John Rosenkilde Nielsen, for his constructive criticisms on reviewing the first drafts; and finally Kristin Rounds, who applied her painstaking editing skills and gave us advice on layout and artwork, all indispensible in getting the work done. We want to thank them for helping us in turning the manuscript into a book.

Peter Beijer
Theo de Klerk

1. What is IT Architecture?

> *Music . . . can name the unnamable and*
> *communicate the unknowable.*
> ~Leonard Bernstein

> *I call architecture frozen music.*
> ~Goethe

The word 'architecture' has many different meanings in the IT World, but the key concepts focus on reducing complexity and on stakeholder consensus of the final result in creating business information systems. Back in 1986 there was already a notion that architecture efforts must be limited in scope and focus on what really matters, something we seem to forget today. We do IT architecture to create business value, not for its own sake. Architecture efforts focus on essentials and are very different from design efforts that are part of IT realization projects. Architecture efforts have a distinct role and precede these projects.

If there is one word in the IT industry that deserves the gold medal of ambiguity, it must be 'architecture.' Especially since the turn of the century, much has been written on the discipline of IT architecture, its concepts, its methodologies, and its value. Sometimes one might get the impression that a religious war of definitions is going on, but this seems normal for a still maturing discipline that found it roots in the mid 1980s. The early software engineering industry needed to capture and explain the software architecture of a system that often had the character of box-and-line diagrams. Eventually the industry started to develop design patterns, styles, best practices, description languages, and formal logic that all influenced the way we practice architecture today. The core aspects of IT architecture are centered on attempts to reduce complexity through abstraction and separation of concerns: abstraction in the sense that the characteristics of the system or artifact are defined without showing the details of construction, and separation of concerns by allowing different domains of interest to have a stake in the final result.

What is IT Architecture?

It was in 1986 that the Partnership for Research in Information Systems Management (PRISM), a multi-client research service of CSC Index, Inc. and Hammer & Company, Inc., developed a powerful architectural model to define the characteristics of information systems in relation to the business.[2] This is an important landmark: the research results emphasized the relation of the business and information technology in the process of architectural developments, and that the scope of architecture should be limited to and focus on what really matters – the business. To integrate business and information technology, the PRISM model for architecture suggested the concept of 'principles' to have a sufficient level of abstraction for the details of construction such that they are specific and distinctive to the organization – just as home builders must relate to the architects, their style preferences, and lifestyles. This usage of principles is fundamentally different from traditional IT architectural approaches. Where many other traditions emphasized standards as the core component of architectures, the PRISM approach focused on the characteristics of the architecture. Throughout this book we will show that applying architectural principles has a big impact on how the concept of architecture is conceived. It deeply influences the view on, for example, traditional requirements engineering, the skills of the architect, and the difference between architecture and design.

The separation of concerns – besides principles, the other core aspect of architecture – goes back to the concept of stakeholder analysis introduced in 1965 by Ansoff to define strategies in improving an organization's strategic position.[3] For most of the strategic management literature, a stakeholder in an organization is broadly defined as 'any group or individual who can affect or is affected by the achievement of the organization's objectives' (Freeman, 1984).[4] The term stakeholder is adopted by the discipline of information systems research. Although definitions of stakeholder vary within this discipline, the literature places the information system, rather than the organization, at the centre of cooperative and competitive interests. Stakeholders can have a different interest in an information system as their point of view differs. Having a different point of view – in short: *view* – is important, to have a comprehensive understanding of the architecture. It goes beyond how many authors equate architecture with system quality attributes (such as reliability and modifiability) and how those attributes are

---

[2] PRISM (1986). *Dispersion and Interconnection: Approaches to Distributed Systems Architecture, Final Report*, June 1986. CSC Index, Inc. and Hammer and Company, Inc. Cambridge MA.

[3] Ansoff, I. (1965). *Corporate Strategy*. New York: McGraw Hill, Inc.

[4] Freeman, R.E. (1984). *Strategic Management: A Stakeholder Approach*. Cambridge, Mass.: Ballinger Publishing Co.

affected by the physical decomposition of the information system in terms of components and their arrangements.

Digital Equipment Cooperation, one of the PRISM research participants, adapted the PRISM model for architecture in 1988 to serve as the basis for its DIGITAL Architecture Review Technique (DART). The key concept here was the use of *principles* and *views* to create abstract descriptions of information systems while simultaneously serving separation of concerns aiming to integrate business goals and information technology. Since then DART continued to evolve into HPGM for ITSA, Hewlett-Packard Global Method for IT Strategy and Architecture.[5]

The two ingredients of architecture – abstraction and separation of concern – gave birth in the mid 1980s to the emerging architectural practices we recognize today. Other frameworks for the development of information systems followed. A well-known example is the Zachman framework for information systems architecture.[6] In 1995 the influence of architecture over the life cycle of a system was greatly recognized, but the concepts of architecture were still not consistently defined and applied within the life cycle of software-intensive systems. To quote the IEEE Software Engineering standards Committee at that time: 'Despite significant industrial and research activity in this area, there is no single, accepted framework for codifying architectural thinking, thereby facilitating the common application and evolution of available and emerging architectural practices.'[7]

In August 1995, the IEEE Architecture Planning Group (APG) was formed and chartered by the IEEE Software Engineering standards Committee (SESC) to set a direction for incorporating architectural thinking into IEEE standards. It took five years to complete the work that is now known as the IEEE-1471-2000 standard titled *IEEE Recommended Practice for*

---

[5] HP Global Method for IT Strategy and Architecture (HPGM for ITSA) has been in use at Digital Equipment Corporation, Compaq Computer Corporation and Hewlett-Packard continuously for over 15 years. It was developed at DIGITAL in the late 1980s as the DIGITAL Architecture and Review Technique (DART), an outgrowth of the PRISM model, developed in 1986 by the Partnership for Research in Information Systems Management (PRISM). DART evolved into the DIGITAL Solution Architecture Technique (DSAT), and after the Compaq acquisition of DIGITAL (Fall 1998) became the Compaq Services Architecture Methodology (CSAM). A key evolution in this was the renaming of the views to the Stakeholder views we know today. With the HP acquisition of Compaq in 2001, CSAM was adopted and integrated into the HPGM family of methods as HPGM for ITSA.

[6] Zachman, J.A. (1987), A framework for information systems architecture, *IBM Systems Journal, vol 26, no. 3, pp. 276-292.*

[7] IEEE. *IEEE Std 1471-2000 - IEEE Recommended Practice for Architectural Description of Software-Intensive Systems, P-iii.* The Institute of Electrical and Electronics Engineers, Inc. 3 Park Avenue, New York, NY 10016-5997, USA.

What is IT Architecture?

Architectural Description of Software-Intensive Systems. Hewlett-Packard (HP) participated in the IEEE-1471 Committee that defined that standard, so there should be no surprise that the definition includes much of what HP already had defined in its approach for architectural descriptions of information systems. The maturing discipline that developed in the industry is now embraced by the IEEE, ISO, the Open Group, HP, IBM, Microsoft, and many others.[8] So today, some standardization can be found in the industry in architectural description of Software-Intensive Systems or Information Systems in general.

Architecture as Essentials

Our brief historical journey through the evolution of architecture teaches us that the grounding principles of IT architecture are about abstraction and separation of concerns. These principles originate from various studies and best practices and standardization work that was done to architecturally describe systems or a system of systems. Considering the genesis of a whole new discipline related to information technology, the question arises what makes architecture so special? And why is it that architecture was (and still is!) so intensively discussed by so many – users, industries and academics?

A possible answer is because IT architecture is about the very essential properties of an information system in its environment. Essential in a sense that if one of the properties is absent, the whole system would collapse. The important thing to note here is that architecture concerns the system in its environment. When we use the word system we embrace the generic system theory (see call-out on system thinking), which deals with a collection of related entities that together realize a certain function. A system refers to an integrated whole with distinctive characteristics that emanate from the relationship among its parts. Integration and coherency are the key aspects in using a systems approach, and one must be aware that these aspects also need a systems approach to have adequate attention. The two go hand in hand, and if we consider information systems as open systems in an environment, we are addressing both the enterprise and its 'ecosystem' when architecturally designing information systems for an enterprise.

Besides a theoretical approach on why architecture is about essentials, perhaps a more practical example will give the reader a 'feeling' for what architecture is addressing. The example is on the evaluation of the business process reengineering (BPR) era. It was the same Thomas Davenport who directed the PRISM initiative that made (self reflecting!) critical notes on the

---

[8] The ISO endorsed IEEE-1471 on July 10, 2007 as ISO/IEC 42010:2007.

mistakes of the BPR movement. One of the recommendations Davenport gave to salvage from the ruins of BPR, as he calls it, was to apply technology only if it is useful to help people to work better and differently.[9] This requires us to have a good understanding of the very essentials of operations where technology needs to be applied, and can add value. IT architecture intrinsically contains the methodological approach to apply information technology such that it serves a purpose; in other words, it addresses the essentials of how IT can help the business processes and the people working with these processes.

> **System Thinking**
>
> The biochemist Lawrence Henderson started using the term 'system' for both living organisms and social structures. From there on, 'system' has been the term used to refer to an integrated whole. Here the distinctive characteristics emanate from the relationship between the parts of the system, and 'system thinking' views a phenomenon as part of a bigger whole. In fact, this is the original meaning of the word 'system,' which is derived from the Greek word 'synhistania' (put together). Understanding things systematically literally means putting things in their context to understand the nature of their interrelationships.
>
> The discovery that systems cannot be understood through analysis (reductionism) was quite a shock for 20th century scientists. The characteristics of its parts do not have the intrinsic characteristics of the system. One can only find the underlying cause of a system within the context of a bigger whole. According to the system approach, we can only understand the characteristics of its parts by studying the organization of the whole. Before studying its building blocks, system thinking first considers the fundamental organization principles. System thinking therefore is very 'contextual' and thus the opposite of analytical (reductionism).

If we take note of the idea that architecture serves a purpose and we move our attention from information technology toward the business it serves, the discussion becomes different. What we are referring to is the concept of strategic alignment, which was originally defined as concerning the inherently dynamic fit between external and internal domains, such as product & market, strategy, administrative structures, business processes and IT (Henderson & Venkatraman 1993).[10] How much more essential can IT architecture be when it deals with information systems and the strategy of the

---

[9] Davenport T.H., (1995), The Fad That Forgot People, *Fast Company, Issue 01, pp. 70.*

[10] Henderson, J.C. & Venkatraman, N., (1993). Strategic alignment: leveraging information technology for transforming organizations. *IBM Systems Journal, 32, 1:4-16.*

firm? Isn't this where we truly explore the shores from both management strategy *and* information technology? We can duly say then that IT architecture builds bridges between the business and IT domain and it inherently becomes a strategic instrument.

Although alignment as a conceptual bridge and the role IT architecture plays therein looks very promising to integrate business and IT, it does bring along a big challenge as the disciplines of strategic management and IT are two very different disciplines. In fact, IT architecture aims to create an objective representation of an information system or IT artifact, but it needs to do this in a world of many different languages, interpretations, and perceptions. This is very challenging, as we are trying to create objectivity in a mind framing subjective world; by definition, these languages do not mix.

In this section, we have questioned why architecture is so intensively discussed by many and explained that our answer is because architecture deals with essentials. An undeniable characteristic of architecture is that it involves both the representation of the essential characteristics of an artifact and the process involved in getting there.[11] Although we have not yet explicitly made a distinct difference between architecture as a process and architecture as an artifact, there is a difference which becomes eminently clear when we inquire into the differences between architecture and design.

How Architecture Differs from Design

As we mentioned earlier, the way people use the word architecture introduces a lot of ambiguity in the IT domain. In the strong emerging profession of architecture, this leads to many discussions which in fact boil down to the distinct difference between architecture and design. There are two ways to look into this difference: as artifact or as process.

From an artifact perspective, we can say that architecture defines the very essential characteristics of an IT solution, information system, and so on. Architecture in that sense is very prescriptive and has its very own mantra: 'everything you need, nothing you don't' to endorse its focus on essentials.[12] This sets architecture apart from design in a sense that architecture 'only' addresses the essential properties and structural constraints to enable decision-making criteria concerning the *goodness* and *completeness* of a solution to a particular problem. Hence, if we consider a different architecture we are

---

[11] Beijer, P. (2005). Architecture Blueprint in Strategic Alignment. Primavera: Program for Research in Information Management. *http://primavera.fee.uva.nl/PDFdocs/2005-12.pd.*

[12] This originated from a marketing tagline from the Nissan ads for the XTerra SUV.

likely solving different problem! In fact, the overarching design question is 'does it work'? whereas the overarching architectural question is 'does it fit'?

One of the key differences here is in the use of principles. Most design methods start from requirements and later develop the specifications and models for the various domains of their specialty – for example, from the requirements for an IT consolidation, through the method's phases, up to the development of specifications and models for servers, storage, network, security, etc. This approach is in contrast to most of the architecture related approaches and methodologies that start with business motivators and strategies. They either use predefined stakeholder views or develop them in the process, and then populate these views with principles to guide the decisions to be made in the more detailed architecture work that follows. The architecture work later serves as guidelines for the design work. Requirements mostly originate from principles. Over time, principles do not change as frequently as requirements do – they are more long term oriented.

Looking at architecture as a process will probably give us a better understanding of how it differs from design. Generally speaking, designing seeks to find optimal solutions to well-understood problems. Design activities are more science than art, algorithmic in nature, and deal mostly with measurable attributes of a system. Architecting, conversely, deals primarily with non-measurable attributes using non-quantitative tools and guidelines based on practical lessons learned – that is, architecture must take a heuristic approach. While design/engineering work is primarily deductive in nature, architecture work is primarily inductive.[13] This does not mean that in architecture quantitative tools and methods are never used, nor that design work never uses a heuristic approach – we just want to highlight the difference in their primary approach. The comparison between architecture and design has been a frequent subject of discussion, possibly because it involves the *raison d'être* of architecture. The key differences between the two were first coined by Fehskens.[14] For our purposes we reformulated them in Table 1. In Chapter 15 on the architecture profession, we will revisit these topics from the perspective of the architect and the designer, i.e. architect*ing* versus design*ing*.

---

[13] Rechtin, E., Maier, M. W. (1997), *The Art of System Architecting*, CRC Press LLC. London. An interesting fact is that the authors commented vehemently on the lack of standardization for definitions in the systems architecture space, and later Marc W. Maier, one of the authors referenced here, helped fix this issue as he was one of the members of the IEEE-1471 Committee.

[14] Fehskens, L (2005), The Architecture of IT Architecture. *Conference proceedings The Open Group Dublin Conference 2005.*
http://archive.opengroup.org/public/member/proceedings/q205/Presentations/fehskens.pdf

What is IT Architecture?

Table 1: The concept of architecture versus design

Architecture	Design
Consists of essentials dictated by needs	Expresses a choice compatible with the architecture
Is rooted in specific needs (different architectures imply different needs)	Can vary but must address the same needs (different designs can satisfy the same needs)
Represents the correct inferences	Documents decisions made
Pursues fit-for-purpose	Represents engineering optimization
Serves business and solution stakeholders	Serves the realization
Concerns the solution in its context	Concerns the construction of solution

In architecture, the essentials of what is being described are dictated by the stakeholder needs and are expressed as principles; in design, however, the choices that are made must be compatible with the defined architecture, thus with how to apply the principles. A different architecture therefore implies that different needs are being addressed – i.e. it solves a different problem. Architecture sets the boundaries or scope for a project. When the time comes to complete the design, different technologies can be considered that address the same need and are within the same scope. (For example, there are many designs/products that address the need for e-mail within an enterprise.)

The role of the architect is mostly to make the right inferences from the stakeholder/business needs that result in an architecture that adequately solves those needs. The designer focuses mostly on making the correct decisions from his rich palette of choices (for example, what technology will work in the environment being designed). Looking at the above, the focus of architecture work is fit-for-purpose, while that of design is optimization.

We have seen in this section that when we talk about architecture, there are always two aspects to bear in mind. On the one hand there is how architecture prescribes the behavior of an IT artifact to solve a known (business) need or problem. On the other hand there is the process of getting there; a process that is highly participative, serving the separation of concerns of the many stakeholders and disciplines involved. Later, we will discuss the architecture profession and elaborate more on the process aspects of architecture.

Conclusion

In this chapter we introduced to the concept of architecture. We have seen that its concepts go back to 1986, when the PRISM research initiative

Conclusion

suggested a model for architecture that emphasized a business justification to the characteristics of enterprise information systems. We showed that architecture is about defining the system characteristics without showing the details of construction and allowing different domains of interest to have a stake in the final result. Stakeholders and architectural principles are paramount in this. This makes architecture very different from design efforts that occur in the follow-on realization project.

The core aspects of IT architecture are centered on the attempts to reduce complexity through abstraction and separation of concerns: abstraction in the sense that the characteristics of the system or artifact are defined without showing the details of construction; separation of concerns by allowing different domains of interest to have a stake in the final result.

2. Applicability of IT Architecture

There are no rules of architecture for a castle in the clouds.
~G.K. Chesterton

Fashion is architecture: it is a matter of proportions.
~Coco Chanel

IT architecture efforts are not always needed for successful IT solutions. The best practice takes away a lot of uncertainties; the need for architecture efforts then depends more on the newness for the organization using the IT solution. Complexity and newness, both in terms of IT and organization, are the factors to take into account to determine whether it is useful to do architecture. Architecture is meaningful in the whole business-IT spectrum. Business architectures can serve innovation. Information architecture emphasizes the effectiveness of information to the business and its processes. Application architectures pursue coherency internally and with other applications. Infrastructure architectures provide the support for business applications and knowledge workers. The idea of solution architecture focuses on coherency with all IT domains (application, infrastructure, etc.) to solve a specific business problem. Architecture on the enterprise level enables integrity of the whole IT landscape of the enterprise.

In the previous chapter we explained that the concept of IT architecture is about reducing complexity through abstraction and separation of concerns, and that its discipline is legitimate because it addresses the essential properties of an information system in its environment. We learned that architecture prescribes how to solve a known (business) need or problem in terms of IT artifacts. But architecture is also characterized by a process that is highly participative in nature, to address the concerns of the many stakeholders and disciplines involved. Two obvious questions then arise:

- When to do architecture – is it always necessary to practice architecture; are there circumstances that can do without architecture?

Applicability of IT Architecture

- Where to apply architecture – do we need to apply architecture in all corners of the information infrastructure (meaning business, applications, infrastructure, and so forth)?

In this chapter we will only look at the applicability questions of architecture from the perspective of the artifacts that need to be created – in other words, the content. The sensemaking participatory process, or put differently, the meaning and value of architecture to the various stakeholders, is discussed in the next chapter.

When to Apply Architecture?

A main objective of IT architecture is to reduce uncertainties by describing the essential properties of a system or solution. These uncertainties can be introduced by the complexity of the 'system' we want to build, but also by the level of newness introduced. In complex systems we typically need to address many parameters, many components, many interfaces to other systems, and so forth. The level of newness can mean that solutions are introduced for the very first time in an environment and therefore require many agreements on its functionality, cooperation, role, parameters, and interfaces, but can also mean many uncertainties in the solution itself, new concepts, interfaces, organizational aspects, etc. We can see both complexity and newness as measures of the difficulty of implementing a system in its environment, as illustrated in Figure 1.

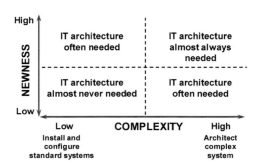

Figure 1: Complexity and newness as a measure for architecture need

Clearly, complex projects do require solid architectures, often done not simply by one architect, but as common practice by a team with complementary subject matter expertise. When new products and/or technologies as well as business and technical complexity are involved, architecture is needed and is a key factor in the success of the solution. This ensures the integration of perspectives through a disciplined approach.

Where to Apply Architecture?

When we ask ourselves where architecture is needed, we are mostly tempted to say anywhere in the spectrum of the business-IT relationship,[15] because it is in this relationship that essentials are paramount, especially the essentials for fit-for-purpose. And as we concluded in the previous chapter, architecture is about essentials! The reality is more subtle, though. We have to consider the areas where design as a follow-on activity after architecture will eventually take place. Basically with architecture we define an information construct that must be unambiguously interpretable such that stakeholders have a good understanding of those parts that serve their needs. The question here is: what is a good understanding? In fact, we look for essential aspects that are *necessary* and *sufficient: necessary* to solve the problem to meet their interest, and *sufficient* to enable decisions to build a solution. Note that this is very different from defining *all* aspects or elements that make up the complete solution – the system as a whole – and in fact goes beyond the architecture definition from IEEE-1471, discussed in the previous chapter.[16]

The IEEE-1471 definition originates from the software industry and is aimed at *software intensive systems*. IT architecture is much more than just software intensive systems; it includes enterprise architecture, business architecture, solution architecture, information architecture, management architecture, and so forth. Architecture affects all layers of business execution and business support in the enterprise, as illustrated in Figure 2. The next sections will go into areas in the business-IT domain that benefit from architecture.

Business

Much has been written on business innovation. Innovation can be seen as exploitation of old uncertainties versus the exploration of opportunities, while setting aside old paradigms.

---

[15] Business could mean the business of an entire enterprise that needs support by Information Technology, but equally well one specific part of a technical infrastructure that needs to serve applications.

[16] IEEE. *IEEE Std 1471-2000 - IEEE Recommended Practice for Architectural Description of Software-Intensive Systems, P-iii*. The Institute of Electrical and Electronics Engineers, Inc. 3 Park Avenue, New York, NY 10016-5997, USA.

Applicability of IT Architecture

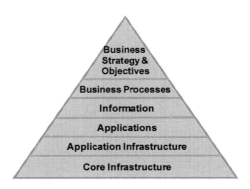

Figure 2: Areas of interest for architecture in the enterprise

To achieve competitive business advantage, companies require acts of innovation according to Michael Porter, one of the most influential thinkers on business strategies.[17] In the 1980s Porter sketched three ways that companies can successfully compete (by cost leadership, differentiation, and focus). Today Porter calls this innovation. Organizations often enlist the help of management consultants to innovate their business. With their expertise to develop structures that affect strategy and industry experience, they pave the path for company innovation. Their design approach is to start from the *general* and go to the *specific*.[18]

We raise the question of whether business can be innovated in a top down design approach as illustrated above – can requirements be the seed of innovation? Moreover, what is it that we actually mean by innovation? Do things better? Do things differently? We argue that a heuristic approach to develop an innovative business is more appropriate. With an architectural approach we have the opportunity to challenge the business (market pull) versus the IT (market push), and vice versa. We can go from the specific to the general such that architecture can contribute in an inductive way to innovate the business. Common problems or challenges are often captured as best practice in architectural models or frameworks. Models and frameworks therefore serve as devices to guide and facilitate the debate about change and not just to describe reality (see Figure 3). For example the eTOM framework,[19] well-known to create enterprise architectures in the telecom industry, is used by many TELCO organizations.

---

[17] Porter, M (1990), Competitive Advantage of Nations, *Harvard Business Review, March-April 1990.*

[18] Kelley, T (1999), Designing for Business – Consulting for Innovation, *Design Management Journal Vol 10, No 3,* Design Management Institute.

[19] Enhanced Telecom Operational Model

Information

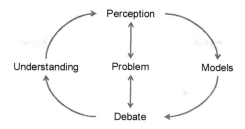

Figure 3: Models as devices for understanding

There is a good case to apply architecture in the business domain. Business architecture, a term frequently used for this,[20] enables us to define the characteristics of the essential elements of an enterprise with regards to its governance, business processes, and information need. It typically covers the primary business functions for the business, how its processes are organized, the knowledge needed, and the organization necessary to run the business. Information technology is an important actor in this spectrum.

Information

Information is the lifeblood of organizations and is a true asset in information intensive enterprises. Information (and its data) does need coherence and reasoning to serve a purpose in an enterprise. Architecture provides the necessary structures that guard the coherency and integrity of data in the enterprise, and it also defines the meaning of information based on the interpretation of various stakeholders in the enterprise. Architecture ensures a meaningful employment of data for the enterprise. Architecture in the information domain addresses the value-add that information can bring to the business and its processes. Information systems, their interoperability, and their structures are typically the artifacts that are subject for discussion in this.

Information as a concept is complex and difficult to grasp. The use of information technology in general is a source of confusion. We tend to see information as a product of technology, while information in essence is human interpretation of objective facts or data. Information assumes a certain level of understanding and interpretation, and it is especially in this context where architecture with its separation of concern and heuristic approach brings insight and value. In fact, the same issues we discussed in

---

[20] See for example the documentation from the Open Group on TOGAF, TOGAF (The Open Group Architecture Framework) Version 8.1 'Enterprise Edition', PART II: Architecture Development Method (ADM), Phase B: Business Architecture.

the previous section on innovation exist in the use and application of information to the business. To answer the question of how we can use information in an effective and innovative manner for the organization, we need the business and the information domain to challenge each other. This is only possible if we can describe the value of information to its stakeholders in a consistent manner – in an architectural way.

The term 'information architecture' is frequently used to address the essential characteristics of how information is used in the organization and organized with systems and applications. As with other architectures, information architecture is closely related to the business processes and bridges the gap to the individual architectures of applications and infrastructures. It covers information, its meaning to the business (human context), the 'systems' that enable information, the types of applications, and data collections that build up these systems.

Applications

Applying architecture to the domain of applications will prevent their characteristics from jeopardizing the existing structure of systems and applications. The structure of the application or application suite needs to be in line with the objectives of the enterprise and the functionalities an application needs to serve to fulfill its purpose therein. There can also be standards defined that are mandatory for applications, the way applications must interoperate, the way applications must fit management frameworks, and any range of necessities that require coherency of the application in its environment.

Complex applications do need guidance for design. They benefit from an approach that explores the possibilities and challenges its structures against what is desired from a functionality perspective with a business purpose. It is clear that with architecture we have an opportunity to address essentialities of the application space within the IT landscape of the enterprise. In fact, architecture is mandatory if we want applications aligned to the development of the business.

Infrastructure

We can see the development of both applications and infrastructures (application and technical) as development of systems that need to be in line with the objectives of the business domain. For the development of technical infrastructures, the same aspects apply as for applications. Technical infrastructures must also develop within a bigger whole and consist of many components that require a coherent deployment. In fact, if we take a deeper look into the concept of infrastructures we will also find that they have additional behaviors next to the pure concept of a system as defined in systems theory.

Infrastructures are connected and interrelated, constituting ecologies of infrastructures. One infrastructure is composed of ecologies of (sub-)infrastructures by building one infrastructure as a layer on top of another, linking logically related networks and integrating independent components, making them interdependent.[21] Infrastructures are more social-technical networks and changes in the components of infrastructures can work out transitively toward other connected infrastructures.

Clearly, the many stakeholders involved with infrastructure development make an appeal to the separation of concerns provided by the concept of architecture. This, together with the way we express architecture through principles, models, and standards, provides a real benefit in managing the complexity of infrastructure development and providing predictability in its performance.

Solutions

It has taken quite a while for the idea of 'solution architecture' to become accepted in the IT industry. Creating solutions to address a problem in the business-IT domain often involves many elements of the IT spectrum (see Figure 2). Therefore, the concept of architecture also applies to the idea of solutions and helps us to create the right ingredients to start a project to solve a problem. Projects in the IT domain facilitate the creation of solutions that solve problems or enable opportunities. As such, projects must fit a business purpose. It is fair to say that IT projects do not exist; there are only business projects!

What constitutes an IT solution? Everything that is needed to completely meet a particular business need in a context. The solution must solve the whole problem and the right problem. If it does not, it may still leave the problem owner unhappy. Many elements can be involved in IT solutions. To name but a few: hardware, off-the-shelf software, custom developed software, systems integration, documentation, project management, organization, governance, financing, training, support, etc. And they can involve the whole spectrum from business initiative down to the IT infrastructure. For example: the implementation of an extra sales channel via the Internet typically involves aspects of business strategies, business

---

[21] Hanseth, O.; Monteiro, E. (1998). Understanding Information Infrastructure. *Manuscript 27. Aug, 1998.* http://www.ifi.uio.no/~oleha/Publications/bok.pdf

processes, information, applications, application infrastructure, and the technical infrastructure. It may even involve new business partners. Orchestrating towards the success of such an endeavor is complex. It is clear that architecture, when done well, can be very effective at helping the stakeholders to understand the critical issues quickly. Solution architecture forms an excellent basis for decision making; it creates 'motional' energy to propel the project-ship.

The Enterprise Context

The discussion up to now demonstrates that the concept of architecture can apply to quite a broad spectrum in the business-IT domain. The business, information, applications, infrastructure, and solutions somehow all address directly or indirectly aspects of the enterprise. When we consider how information technology is more and more intertwined with the processes that drive the enterprise, it doesn't take much imagination to see that there is a growing need for coherency among the various domains of architecture we have discussed until now. That is not easy. The business, information, applications, infrastructure, all have different dynamics and life spans. Each used in isolation may end up producing another stove-pipe in the enterprise – regardless how productive it may be.

Architecture on the enterprise level enables us to create structures for a system of systems such that we can maintain the coherency and integrity of the whole IT landscape of the enterprise. Its goal is to define what kinds of applications, systems, infrastructure, etc. are relevant to the enterprise and what applications, systems, and so forth the enterprise needs in order to run the business. We have to realize that all IT elements in the enterprise have a different purpose; some might have not so obvious functions and less direct effect, while others are key on the enterprise performance. Enterprise architecture helps us to define and maintain the IT essentialities at the highest level of abstraction possible, such that it enables guidance for lower level IT related implementations of systems, applications, infrastructures, and so forth.

We frequently use the term *enterprise* for various levels of abstraction. With *enterprise* we sometimes mean a corporation, a federation, a division, a department, a business, etc., but the term may also refer to a county, a country, or a region. It is not uncommon to use the term *enterprise* when we point to a single division or business unit instead. Especially when the type of business very much differs between divisions, and as a result their IT has no relation, it makes sense to have various enterprise architectures. This raises some important points when discussing the scope of an enterprise architecture: what is the level of detail and breadth addressed? Does it comprise the whole enterprise or parts thereof? Does it address just one architecture domain, in detail, for the whole enterprise and its parts? Does it address all architecture domains in detail? Does it address all architecture domains broadly? The definition of enterprise architecture has been ambiguous and the conventional wisdom is rapidly becoming that enterprise architecture is more than enterprise IT architecture.[22] It is therefore sometimes more appropriate to speak of enterprise IT architecture or enterprise level architectures instead of the enterprise architecture, all depending on the IT domains, scope and breadth we encounter. Figure 4 illustrates some of the ways the domains (and their architectures, as was shown in Figure 2) can relate to each other.

The concept of enterprise architecture inherently carries the risk of seeing the enterprise as a system to be architected and subsequently designed and built. This is very misleading and results in tragic mistakes and waste of effort. An enterprise architecture needs to be fit-for-purpose, which is the system that guides the systems; put differently, to guide and direct the architectures that really make things happen. As such, enterprise architectures are seldom

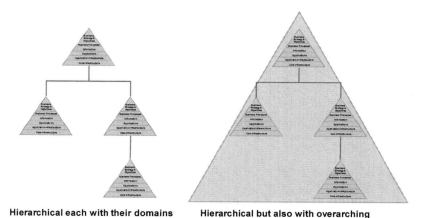

Hierarchical each with their domains   **Hierarchical but also with overarching enterprise architecture**

Figure 4: Hierarchies of areas of interest for architecture in the enterprise

---

[22] Fehskens (2008) states in his presentation *Re-Thinking Architecture* held at The Open Group Conference Toronto 2008: "There's a lot more to an enterprise than its IT; IT budgets represent about 2% of revenues. An increasing number of enterprise architects believe that the rest of the enterprise, often generically referred to as 'the business', should be architected as well. To address the architectures of things outside the domain of IT, we need a concept of architecture that is not technological, and that is expressed in nontechnical language."

See *http://www.opengroup.org/conference-live/doc.tpl?CALLER=documents.tpl&dcat=57&gdid=17752*

Applicability of IT Architecture

created from scratch and exclusively top-down. Executing a 'labeling exercise' by filling in an architecture framework with the as-is situation is also a waste of effort. Meaningful enterprise architecture initiatives pursue coherency among the various architecture domains against the background of business developments, i.e. the to-be situation. An enterprise architecture is the result of careful balancing enterprise and solution based initiatives. Enterprise architectures mature over time.

Tying It Together

We can conclude that in any area that demands a well-defined structure with essential elements, architecture is the appropriate way to overcome communication gaps in the spectrum of the business-IT relationship. Architecture finds its way into many domains that constitute the information technology of the enterprise. Structural coherency among the business, the information, and the technology is a necessity to create sufficient positive value to the enterprise with IT: first to be effective in the ecosystem that an enterprise is part of, and second to be efficient in the processes it encompasses. Figure 5 depicts where architecture is beneficial for the various domains within the enterprise.

The idea of business-IT alignment is frequently used in attempts to implement information technology such that it is properly aligned to the needs of the enterprise. What that means practically is that the information infrastructure – the whole of information, applications, technology, people, procedures, and facilities – is durably structured to cope with any future change in the relation between the business domain and the IT domain. Architecture serves that purpose.

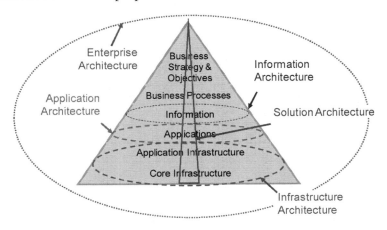

Figure 5: Architecture in various domains within the enterprise

Conclusion

In this chapter we explained when to do architecture and where in the business-IT spectrum we can apply architecture. We learned that it is not always necessary to do architecture, as it all depends on complexity and newness with respect to both IT solutions and organization. Architecture can be used in all domains we recognize in the business-IT relation – the enterprise. This concerns, for example, business processes, information, application, and core infrastructure. Besides that, it is an instrument to the essential properties of systems or sub-systems in the enterprise, and it is a good communication instrument as it creates shared understanding among stakeholders. Architecture aims at addressing the appropriate things in the whole spectrum of the information infrastructure to maximize business value.

3. The Value of IT Architecture

> *IT architecture is more than abstract boxes and diagrams;*
> *it is a participatory sensemaking process that*
> *includes the subtle wealth of meaning.*
>
> ~Peter Beijer

It is often questioned whether it pays off to perform architecture. We argue that architecture creates value to the business and saves money from trial-and-error by doing the right thing. Architectural efforts are aimed at fit-for-purpose and beneficial to the business sponsors, the users of IT, and the IT practitioners. However, architecture has different meanings hence values to these actors. This concerns not only the form, the matter, and the processes of the IT solutions we architect, but also all those immaterial aspects such as meaning, politics, culture, behavior, intentions, objectives, etc.

We have seen in the previous chapter that the concept of architecture can be applied in various areas of the IT spectrum, such as information, applications, and infrastructure, and that it has an innovation potential in the business domain. Both the business and IT domains can benefit from having a heuristic approach to solve the coherency puzzles for IT-related structures that many organizations face when trying to deploy information and its related technology.

Applying abstracts of coherent structures is one thing, and whether it also helps the organization to make progress in their business objectives is another issue. A very valid question here is: Why would a business sponsor bet his money on architecture to get a very functionally – to the business – furnished IT environment? Popularly said, is it worth the effort? With the same validity, the users of the IT can raise similar questions: Is it worth the effort to invest in architecture efforts to get the job done better? Said differently, can architecture represent the users' concerns in using the IT environment appropriately? Aside from sponsors and users, we could question whether architecture has any value to IT practitioners. Is there a benefit in using architecture for the follow-on design and implementation processes that IT practitioners face? At some point in time, technology has to be deployed; the obvious question is, whether architecture helps the designer, the builder, and the project manager to make the right choices in this. In this chapter we will answer these questions.

About Value

The central question we address in this chapter is whether it is worth the effort to do IT architecture. If we look at problems in the context of the enterprise from a holistic systems perspective, the answer is quite obviously 'yes', because it helps us to structure a solution within this 'system.' This was our point of departure in the previous chapter, when we looked from an IT perspective at the whole spectrum of the enterprise – from business 'down' to IT infrastructure. This concerns very much the form, the matter, and the processes of the IT solutions we architect. An additional dimension to this comprises all those immaterial aspects we will encounter when practicing architecture, such as meaning, politics, culture, behavior, intentions, objectives, etc. Some call this the social dimension, a dimension where rationality has another order and is a natural part of the architecture process. It has much to do with meaning and sense making because an organization is more than just an abstract entity that can be modeled according to clear-cut principles and we cannot put the subtle wealth of meaning of an organization into XML, UML or any sort of formal expression.[23]

Every affected party has its own value judgment that is subjective and can be very unreasonable, illogical, or incomprehensible to others. This intrinsic force-field 'under the hood' can be quite challenging sometimes, but it is typical. To address the separation of concern – a primary characteristic to create fit-for-purpose architectures – through architecture views, it is an essential condition that there is involvement from all those parties. We will revisit architecture views in Chapter 6.

This all justifies architecture as a participatory and heuristic process and goes far beyond what the IEEE was aiming for with the IEEE-1471 standard in their search for an '[. . .] accepted framework for codifying architectural thinking [. . .]' as we discussed in Chapter 2.[24] The key message here is that having an architecture framework that codifies essential system properties is not enough. A well-defined sensemaking approach is necessary to construct a meaningful IT solution that serves all interests and fits its

---

[23] Maes, R., & Vries de, E. J. (2008). Information Leadership: The CIO as Orchestrator and Equilibrist. *Twenty Ninth International Conference on Information Systems. Paris.*

[24] IEEE Std 1471-2000 - *IEEE Recommended Practice for Architectural Description of Software-Intensive Systems*, P-iii. The Institute of Electrical and Electronics Engineers, Inc. 3 Park Avenue, New York, NY 10016-5997, USA.

purpose: the business (i.e. we have a good architectural fit). In the next sections we will visit each type of interest individually: the sponsors, the users, and the IT practitioners, and elaborate on what architecture brings them.

Value to Sponsors

Sponsorship for architecture endeavors can be found within the IT domain, the business domain, in fact anywhere in the organization. This individual – the sponsor – has direct or indirect responsibility for the costs made. Although many stakeholders are involved, he is the one most interested in the final architecture results. The challenge every sponsor faces is not only whether the architected solution is appropriate to solve his problem, but also whether it is supported by the organization. A well-defined architecture methodology will guard the sponsor from both. It will ensure that IT artifacts are not created without reason; every single element of an IT solution has a reason to be present and needed. We will see later that there are some very distinct aspects in HP's architecture approach that will prevent so-called technocratic hobby-horses, and only strive for solutions that fit a defined purpose.

An important factor to gain organizational commitment for an IT solution is that all relevant parties have an interest in the development of the IT architecture. In practice, this means that many parties can be involved, and this can often lead to weakly defined architectures where one tries to please all, to run with the hare and hunt with the hounds, as the saying goes. Architecture is about essentialities that lead to the proper choices. The architecture approach keeps the major issues separated from minor issues and allows consideration what is desirable versus what is feasible. Even though there can be many direct stakeholders, with some effort consensus is achievable. If not, the approach goes back to essentialities, eventually to the business stakeholder to reformulate the problem at hand.

Another key value that architecture brings to the sponsor is that it gives them an 'artist's impression' of the solution, especially with respect to correctness and completeness. Scoping the topics of interest up-front in an architecture engagement also gives the sponsor insight on whether there is potential for the necessary collaboration among the stakeholders to complete the endeavor. In fact, the sponsor gains good insight about whether the potential solution is going to make sense, rooted in the business case, and is feasible at all. This is a very effective means to take go/no-go decisions based on main points of interests. This approach follows a short-term initial architectural concept to allow this decision.

The Value of IT Architecture

Value to Users

Change is a challenge for most people. For the users of an IT solution, it is even more of a challenge as they have the responsibility to deliver production-ready work. If the IT solution is of bad quality – in the broadest sense – it can jeopardize their current activities or make it difficult for them to contribute to the new goals of the enterprise when the new business solution is implemented. Users make or break the 'system.' Through the architecture process, they can get upfront information about the objectives of the new solution and they can provide their experience of how things are meant to work before they are actually built. Users are very valuable in this process as they are the ones who know the existing processes and their relationships. In the case of a new solution they should be able to visualize from a user perspective what is needed to solve the problem. Users have the chance to bring in experience of how work-streams can be optimized.

Value to Practitioners

IT practitioners, whether they are the ones that architect, develop, implement, operate, or maintain the IT solution, all benefit from an architectural approach. We have seen that architecture is applicable on various levels of abstraction like business, information, technology, and even the whole of a solution, including project and operational aspects. This provides room for layered approaches as higher level or overarching enterprise architectures can be 'incarnated' in the final solution. This also makes intradepartmental and interdepartmental participation possible, making the concept of architecture a truly enterprise-wide instrument that is capable of aligning solutions to various business related problems as well as beyond the enterprise such as clients, partners and regulators. Even solutions in federated environments can benefit from this approach.

Very often we see that technology endeavors are very paper consuming projects that create pure bureaucracy that is counterproductive to the business. Organizational resistance against architecture (the *architecture police*) can be one of the effects. Most likely the business people are negatively biased against architecture. A proper architecture approach that includes a strong principle driven approach with a seamless chain of justification of the whole solution spectrum the architecture has to cover – from business 'down-to' technology – will induce motional energy. This truly is a virtue of solution architecture and will motivate all stakeholders involved; or at least comes down to the essence to solve any serious roadblocks ahead.

Another advantage of architecture for practitioners is that, by definition, architecture can be vendor neutral. Architecture is about principles, models, and standards that can be created without any vendor bias. Decisions on technology can be left until farther down the path where the design work starts. In contrast, when there are any enterprise standards for technology, they can be imposed upon design work through the help of architecture. Architecture gives both room and constraints to follow-on implementation work, for the benefit of all – to stay on track to fulfill business needs.

Handover of concepts and ideas that the architecture articulates is done gradually along the architecture process. Practitioners are very important stakeholders in an architecture engagement, as they are close to technical feasibilities. Aside from being a necessity in the architecture process, their involvement very naturally results in a gradual handover between architecture and realization project instead of a handover that happens at a single point in time. It is important to remember that handover is not a moment in time, but a carefully orchestrated process.

Conclusion

Architecture efforts have a value to different actors in the business-IT relation, but that value is perceived differently from one actor to another. For business sponsors, architecture gives early insight about whether a solution is appropriate to solve the problem and whether the IT solution is worth the money. IT users can bring in their best practice to ensure that the solution meets the business (process) needs they are involved in, and IT practitioners can justify IT solutions to the business and create the proper circumstances to start realization projects.

4. Overview of HPGM for ITSA

> *There are no easy methods of learning difficult things;*
> *the method is to close your door, give out that*
> *you are not at home, and work*
>
> ~Joseph de Maistre

HP's architecture methodology, 'HP Global Method for IT Strategy and Architecture' – 'HPGM for ITSA' or 'ITSA' for short – is used to elaborate on key aspects of IT architecture and how to practice it. In the ITSA framework the different stakeholders are represented by the business view, the functional view, the technical view, and the implementation view. The organization's interests are expressed as business drivers and business goals, the stakeholder interests in principles, models, and standards. The ITSA framework is the foundation for the architecture concept (a first draft) and the fully elaborated architecture blueprint.

In the previous chapters we discussed what we mean by architecture, where architecture is applicable, and what the value of architecture is to sponsors, users, and practitioners. Until now we have looked at architecture as a concept and discussed how it is unique compared to other development activities (such as design). Moreover architecture is necessary and essential to successfully define artifacts that can really be built and implemented. In addition, we looked at why architecture is indispensable to align information technology to the way business executes, hence defining something that serves a purpose.

We can conclude that architecture is a necessary activity in complex situations precursory to realizations (design, build, implement, manage, etc.) and that it serves a business purpose. We will elaborate on key aspects of IT architecture and how to practice it. We do this against the background of HP's architecture methodology, HP Global Method for IT Strategy and Architecture – HPGM for ITSA, or ITSA for short. The way that ITSA is organized lays the foundation to both define artifacts and to serve a purpose. This chapter introduces the way ITSA is structured and how it is deployed.

The Architecture Framework

A core characteristic of ITSA is that it is a stakeholder driven approach. The underlying architecture framework (the ITSA framework) is defined such that architectural elements are expressed by using stakeholder representation. If we were to just look at the business domain and the IT domain, two stakeholders would come to mind; a) the business stakeholder who aims for the best business results and b) the IT stakeholder, who proposes the art of the possible with information technology. However, there is much more at stake.

Deploying IT solutions that are cumbersome to work with would frustrate the eventual user and would seriously degrade overall performance, and likely jeopardize the organization's reputation. This is why the user of the IT solution is also a genuine stakeholder. Additionally, if it would take an immense effort to realize a solution, one could question whether deploying a 'simpler' one would be more sensible – after all, our objective should not be the best solution but the right solution unless we are running some architectural beauty contest. We do see now that another stakeholder surfaces: the one who implements the solution.

We recognize four types of stakeholders: the business sponsor, the user, the technician, and the implementer. Each of these stakeholders matches with what we call an architectural view: the business view, the functional view, the technical view, and the implementation view, as shown in Table 2.

Table 2: The four architecture views

Business view (Why?)	From a sponsor's perspective, the business context is explored. What are the internal and external motivations? Who participates in the business processes? What are the project goals? How is success measured? What is the value chain? Why is it good for the business? Etc.
Functional view (What?)	From a user's perspective, we determine what the solution must do. What is the user doing? What services are provided? What is the flow and ownership of information? What is its required quality? Etc.
Technical view (How?)	From a constructor's perspective, the structure of the solution is defined. How do we interface among different parts? How do we exchange data? Which applications are used? What is the required quality? Etc.
Implementation view (Wherewith?)	From a realization perspective, the solution items are justified for implementation. How are solutions tested and accepted? How are financials secured? How are organizational aspects secured? Etc.

The Architecture Framework

Now that we have defined the four angles from which we can describe architecture elements, let us define what it takes to express architecture. The fundamental ITSA architectural elements include business drivers, business goals with business metrics – they are closely associated with the business view – and principles, models, and standards. Each of the four views has its own principles, models, and standards. Together they make up the architecture of a coherent solution. What we mean by these architecture elements is discussed in detail in later chapters. For now, it is sufficient to define:

- **Business drivers** are business conditions, pressures, or opportunities that motivate to seek a solution.

- **Business goals** are objectives of the solution, i.e. what the solution must accomplish for the business and actually justifying its costs.

- **Business metrics** define the goals in measurable terms so they indicate the degree to which goals are achieved.

- **Principles** are a fundamental approach or means for achieving a goal; they are timeless, show how the solution is meant to work, and constrain decisions about the solution and its realization.

- **Models** represent essential properties of some aspect(s) the solution; they promote understanding by making important things obvious and facilitate reasoning about the solution (analysis).

- **Standards** are well-defined conventions or measures with which a solution must comply; they are used to constrain and/or evaluate the development and implementation of a solution.

Figure 6 illustrates the four views and their architecture elements.

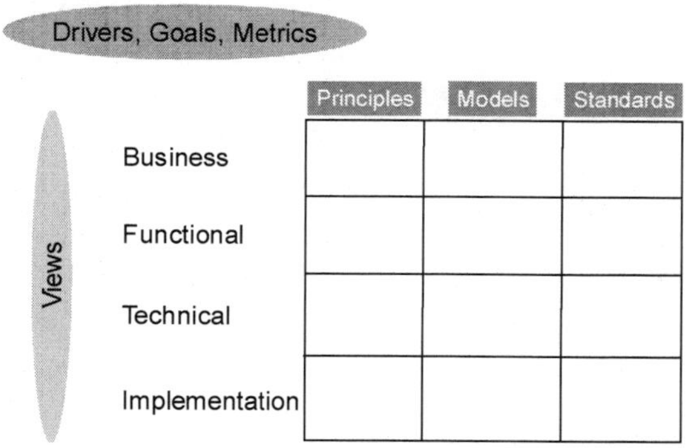

Figure 6: The four views with architectural elements

Overview of HPGM for ITSA

When we talk about defining architecture for a solution, we actually mean that we go through all the four views and define principles, models, and standards. Before doing so, business drivers, goals, and metrics are needed to secure that the solution we define is in line with the problem (the business); hence the solution serves the purpose of solving these problems.

The ITSA Framework

The ITSA framework we introduced above is fundamental in the methodologies to create IT architectures. The framework can be seen as the unifying mechanics to create architectural elements in the methodologies: the Architecture Concept and the Architecture Blueprint. As Figure 7 illustrates, the ITSA framework serves at the foundation to create coherent content for the ITSA architecture methodologies, as well as other methodologies. Let us take a closer look at the methodologies.

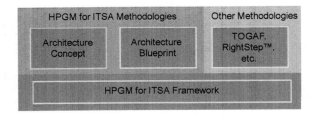

Figure 7: The ITSA framework as foundation for methodologies

The Architecture Concept Methodology

The architecture concept develops the content of the ITSA framework to express the architecture in principles, models, and standards, organized as four interlinked views (business, functional, technical, and implementation). The concept is developed with intensive stakeholder interaction, usually in a workshop format, but individual interviews combined with desk research are also a viable way to create an architecture concept.

The Architecture Blueprint Methodology

The architecture blueprint further elaborates the concept's framework into the architecture blueprint deliverables: Solution Overview, Architectural Requirements, Features and Functions, Architectural Design, Acceptance Criteria, Feasibility Assessment, and a Plan. Together these deliverables

Conclusion

provide the basis for development and deployment of the solution. The methodology is set up such that it:

- Develops a necessary and sufficient ('everything you need and nothing you don't') representation of the architecture of a solution to a specific business problem, need, or opportunity (which may entail clarifying and articulating that problem, need, or opportunity).

- Develops among the solution's stakeholders a shared understanding of and commitment to a problem, need, or opportunity and the architecture of its solution.

The sponsor of the architecture endeavor can use the architecture deliverables of the architecture blueprint to submit a Request for Proposal (RFP) for realization of the IT solution. Later, we will discuss these deliverables in more detail.

Other Frameworks and Methodologies

In practice many architecture methods and frameworks are used such as The Open Group Architecture Framework (TOGAF), RightStep™, the Zachman Framework, Gartner's Architecture Framework, etc. An approach which emulates fundamental properties of group theory allows for the use of the ITSA methodology and its framework to develop and populate architectural descriptions within other frameworks. This provides a significant number of important features not available in other frameworks and methods. It improves the quality and consistency of the resulting architectural description.[25] Later we will describe how the mechanics of the ITSA framework enable us to consistently develop high level architectural descriptions using the ITSA methods.

Conclusion

In this chapter we showed the basic elements of the ITSA framework and methodologies. Stakeholder representation is provided through the four ITSA views. Stakeholders interest are expressed through principles, models, and standards in each of the views. Business drivers, business goals, and metrics are overarching and make the architecture serve a (business) purpose.

---

[25] Rivera, R (2009). Mapping one architecture framework into another by emulating group theory. *Research Disclosure Journal, May 2009 pp. 527*.

5. Business Drivers and Goals

Take care of the sense and the sounds will take care of themselves
~ Lewis Carroll

The factors that strongly motivate an IT-related change are called business drivers. They express the pain, opportunity, or any directive that an organization primarily needs to address. The business goals and their associated metrics express what must be achieved through an IT solution to solve the 'problem' as stated in the business driver. The metrics ensure that the goals are defined in clear and measurable terms.

It may sound as a trivial statement: 'whatever IT solution is created, it must support the enterprise business goals in an efficient and effective way'. Why else would we do it? Apparently for lots of reasons that remain unspoken. The history of IT is filled with solutions that were considered nice to have, not-so essential and that have cost lots of money but without delivering much to the enterprise goals.

It is very easy for this to happen. What is essential for one person or stakeholder may not be relevant to another. And if none has a firm grip on or understanding of the enterprise objectives, it is very easy to make the wrong decision and sub-optimize. Why else do we see many SOA-related projects while the service orientation is only a valid choice for a number of organizations but doesn't bring much to others? Why are there always new IT buzzwords that seem to cure all problems, only not to deliver on their promises? And if they do, they replace the original problems by others. There simply is no single answer to all problems. To address them in an effective manner, we need a deep understanding of the problems and the options available. Only then it is possible for us to make the best choice from the available options to fit your needs. This is where architecture helps: by associating business goals and drivers with an IT architecture that fits and makes sense to the business.

The root cause for every IT solution lies within business drivers and goals, the topics for this chapter. They justify any architectural element through which we express architecture: the principles, models, and standards. The latter are topics for follow on chapters.

Business Drivers

The slogan of an American fitness equipment manufacturer is: 'no pain, no gain.' In other words, nothing comes for free; to be in better shape, we need to work for it. In our dynamic world where new innovations are developed, new competitors are always on the move to eat away market share, even well shaped organizations cannot rest on their laurels for any long period of time. They need to be vigilant and constantly assess their position and market offering and go with the flow, or even better, stay ahead of the flow. In the competitive global world, enterprises try to stay on top of the competition through better service, better products, better quality for the lowest possibly expenses and with a proper value/price ratio.

As soon as figures drop (or are anticipated to drop), it is time for action. This situation drives the organization to change its offering or operational model. Some of these changes need to be implemented in the supporting IT environment. For some people, IT may only be supportive (such as doing the bookkeeping), but increasingly IT is an empowering, enabling factor, allowing unique services or different, better services than those offered by the competition. This is also true if the core business of the organization is to provide IT services, as is the case for organizations that facilitate outsourcing as a differentiating factor, IT solutions must be put to use as soon as there are indications that the organization needs to change its ways. These indications are called business drivers. A business driver in ITSA is defined as:

> A business driver is a business condition or pressure that motivates the client to seek a solution.

ITSA recognizes three types of business drivers:

- **Pain** – external situations are hurting the organization and causing loss of market share, revenue, or profit. Signs are typically reduced orders or profit, higher costs, fewer customers, not offering services customers are looking for and which they can get from the competition, not being able to stay with the game.

- **Directive** – legal or regulatory requirements that force the organization to adjust its way of working. These requirements must be complied with, or the organization will face the risk of not being able to continue business. Fortunately, directives hurt all organizations in the same market. But becoming compliant may be easier for some than others. Examples are Sarbanes-Oxley or

Basel II compliance, US Food and Drug Administration (FDA) requirements, environmental standards.

- **Opportunity** – a new market is spotted, a new service or product is developed that is not currently offered by others and that is likely to become high in demand, an existing service can be reshaped into a more attractive proposal. But also new acquisitions may open new frontiers to an existing organization that make it a bigger player in its market or open up new markets.

Although the examples used in the three types of business drivers are of a commercial nature, the business condition or pressure is not necessarily limited to commercially oriented organizations. Non-profit organizations, and also governmental organizations, can equally well experience a pain, directive, or opportunity. For example, governmental organizations have to deal with operational efficiency (policy objectives, public private partnerships, costs, etc.), political return (transparency, accountability, greater participation, etc.), and constituent services (constituent value, effective interactions, single point of contact, etc.).[26]

Business drivers must be identified properly before attempting to develop any solution or architecture that will contribute to the organization's well being. Identification of drivers is not normally the task of the IT architect; s/he merely verifies them to kick-start the architecture process. Drivers are identified by the company's CEO, board of directors, the stakeholders themselves. Drivers will substantiate why IT solutions are needed and therefore IT architecture comes into play. Depending on the type of drivers, the IT solution architecture may need to focus on addressing issues that affect the entire enterprise or just a division or department of it.

In some cases, organizations consider this information strategic and will not make it public; they will keep it within small circles of people. The IT architect may not be familiar with or recognize these drivers. That should not be a problem, as long as those drivers do translate to a set of business goals the organization has set out for itself to be achieved in a reasonable timeframe and with positive business impact. It is on these goals that the IT architecture is based, as we will see in the following section.

---

[26] Kost, J., & Di Maio, A. (2003). *Creating a Business Case for a Government IT Project,* Gartner Research, Stanford Connecticut.

Business Goals

Where business drivers are (external) factors, forcing the organization to change its conduct, business goals are set by the organization itself, mostly by management. Mission statements, vision workshops and other business-oriented approaches are all good opportunities and sources to define business goals. The key message here is that business goals are a controlled response from the organization to the uncontrolled business drivers. Business goals formulate intentions of the company to develop solutions that address the drivers: relieve the pain, comply with rules or offer and enable the new opportunities. A business goal in ITSA is defined as:

> A business goal is an objective of the solution: what the solution must accomplish in business terms.

Obviously, a single business driver may result in several business goals. Similarly, a single business goal may address multiple business drivers. It is important to be aware of the adjective *business* in business goal. It is very easy to define many goals that an organization or one of its divisions should strive for. However, the ultimate aim is to make an organization more successful. For commercial enterprises, this results in more profit or market share. For non-commercial organizations, it translates into better or more efficient services as well as market share. The business goals, therefore, are all aimed at improving or changing the *business* of the organization.

Special attention and awareness is needed in identifying proper business goals. The introduction of a new service process, a new sales channel, or a new web portal may at first seem to be a proper business goal. But they are not. Ask the question 'why is this new sales channel (or process or portal) helping to solve the organization's predicament?' The answer will likely be that it will help to improve sales or services. Then *those* are the real business goals. We may need to ask the 'why?' question repeatedly to get to the fundamental business goal. Ultimately, the final 'why?' question answer lies in the realm of the business drivers (see Figure 8).

For example, if we ask 'why do you want to improve sales?' the answer might be: 'because sales are currently not going well and we notice it by dropping sales or patronage' – a clear business driver of the *pain* category. The earlier, one-but-last answer to the repeated *why* question is closest to the formulation of a business goal.

The earlier formulations of candidate business goals that we rejected imply a choice made in response to the realization of the real business goal. In the example above, the following steps are made:

Business Goals

- We are driven to do something about declining sales (business driver).

- We set ourselves a goal of improving sales (business goal) by 5% over the next 6 months (business metric – to be discussed in the next section).

- We decide (make a choice) that the best way to do this is by introducing a new sales channel using a new web portal (business principle – to be discussed in the next chapter).

The business choice we made in the last step is one out of the myriad of possible choices available to the stakeholders of the organization. The choice made however, is the one best fitting for the organization according to its stakeholders. Other organizations may decide on different choices based on the decisions made by their stakeholders. Each organization has its unique combination of culture, (management) structure, history, capability, flexibility, and assets. These ensure that the organization makes the most fitting and organically natural choices. In the next chapter we will see that such a business choice is in fact a business principle – an important element of the IT architecture we define.

Figure 8: Business drivers, goals and choices

When IT-oriented people are asked about business goals, chances are that they will give IT-related answers. Such answers may include replacement or development of an IT solution. Suggestions may include restructuring the data center, reducing the time it takes to store a database record, or implementing a service oriented architecture.

Business Drivers and Goals

The CEO, sales force, customer-facing staff that actually perform the business of the organization, as well the customers to whom they provide the service or sales, either don't know how IT supports their business or don't care – as long as IT does what it supposed to do. That this support translates into having a clustered server configuration or optimized order database is quite possible. But these are IT goals which are subservient to the business goals and they are not business goals by themselves.

Even for organizations that specialize in outsourcing, the business goals are not IT related. Their client's core business may be the production and selling of shoes or pizzas, using outsourced IT as an enabler (in the order fulfillment cycle). The outsourcing organization's core business is providing those enabling IT services. Its goals, however, are in the realm of doing this efficiently and to the client's satisfaction at an acceptable price. It is up to the outsourcing organization to decide what is the best way for them to reach these goals (for example, by standardizing IT services and service agreements) – choices that are embedded in their business principles.

In summary, be very wary of any business goal specified in any other language than that used by business people – it may well be stating a choice or sub-goal as a result of a business goal and not a valid goal at all. These choices we will see later to be (business) principles.

Business Metrics

Goals are set to be met, but when do we know a goal has been met? Politically talented individuals have a way of defining goals in obscure ways so that there is always a way to explain why they have been reached – even if they haven't. For business goals, there should be no doubt about what is meant exactly by a goal and when it is met. For this reason, each business goal is associated with one or more metrics that specifically state the conditions that must be satisfied to reach that business goal. This may also imply that some baseline measurements must be made in the current environment in order to compare those measurements with the ones made after the solution is put in place and made operational. The metrics set for business goals need to be SMART:[27]

---

[27] Caution! The SMART acronym is used by many, and we all probably have a hunch of what we mean by it. However, depending on the context, it has many different meanings, and therefore any reference to SMART must always must be accompanied a proper explanation of the acronym.

- **Specific** – only clear definitions of goals ensure that everyone is on the same page and understands the same outcome as a result. There is no confusion about what the goal represents.
- **Measurable** – based on the clear specification, it must be possible to define criteria that indicate when a goal is reached. By when, by whom, by what measurement. This avoids vague goals such as 'first customer choice,' unless one clearly defines how this is measured.
- **Achievable** – the goal must be within reach and power of the organization's resources and capabilities.
- **Realistic** – goals must be concrete and within the control span of the organization.
- **Time bound** – the goal must be achievable within a reasonable time span so there is a sense of urgency and commitment to reach the goal.

When looking for metrics, it helps to focus on areas such as quality, agility, risks, and costs. It is preferable to have concrete business goals. And even somewhat vaguely formulated goals can be made concrete by attaching metrics to them. As an example, the vague business goal, 'be the number 1 supplier for shoes within the next 2 years' (which seems more like a mission statement), can be made acceptable as a business goal as soon as the company agrees on what this means and how it is measured. A business metric to this goal can be specified as: 'The annual market research XYZ states that 30% of buyers of shoes do it in our shops.' This metric meets the SMART criteria:

- Specific – research XYZ provides the answers.
- Measurable – 30% of buyers of shoes.
- Achievable – XYZ does the research annually and is not likely to stop this.
- Realistic – the industry segment trusts the objectivity of the data by XYZ and we already have 20% of the buyers; an increase of 10 seems realistic enough.
- Time bound – within 2 years from now.

So we prefer concrete business goals. Business goals are low in number; three to six is typical. When there are many business goals, the real essential goal, the common root of several of the given business goals, probably has

Business Drivers and Goals

been overlooked. The 'why' question will help to identify the real goals. Some example business goals are:

- The process from order to delivery of a book must complete within two days.
- Financial reporting must be available and actual to within 1 week of sales.
- Customer complaints are dealt with within 2 days and closed to their satisfaction within a week for 90% of all cases.

Business goals will be the starting point for the IT architecture. They determine how the organization will focus its activities on realizing its objectives. Business goals will influence the principal decisions and architectural elements that underpin the IT solution. (Architectural elements will be discussed in later chapters.) While business drivers may not be communicated widely, the business goals must be known – at least those that have an effect on the IT solutions for which we are to formulate the IT architecture. Without business goals, it is impossible to justify choices in the architecture process. We can say that business drivers, goals, and metrics inspire or motivate the creation of architectural elements in the architecture framework, as illustrated in Figure 9.

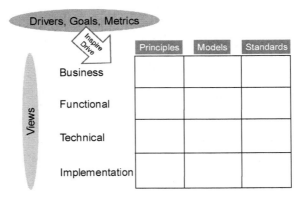

Figure 9: Business goals drive the architecture

Business drivers and goals, if not yet clearly defined, can be elicited through various tools that are used in the discipline of strategic management. Tools that are frequently used are the SWOT (Strength, Weakness, Opportunity and Threat) analysis and the Balanced Score Card. Both these tools, and how they can be beneficial in the architecture process, are discussed in Appendices A and B.

Conclusion

In this chapter, we introduced the first elements of the ITSA framework: business drivers, business goals, and metrics. The root cause for every IT solution lies within business drivers and goals. They express the pain, opportunity, or directive that the IT solution needs to solve, and as such provide the justification for IT needs.

6. Stakeholders and Views

> *Every step of progress the world has made has been from scaffold to scaffold, and from stake to stake*
> ~Wendell Phillips

> *The house does not frame the view: it projects the beholder into it.*
> ~Harwell Hamilton Harris

Various stakeholders in organizations have a vested interest in an IT solution (or not!). Architecture considers this by looking from four different angles to the situation. These so-called views represent the business, the user, the constructor, and the builder. In ITSA we call them the business view, functional view, technical, and implementation view, respectively. Agility, quality, costs, and risks are typical subjects where stakeholders can have opposing interests when considering an IT solution. A careful balancing act is needed to ferret out the essentials in each of the views and create consensus among the stakeholders.

In the previous chapter we looked at the root for any IT initiative: the business drivers and business goals. Once these are identified, there is no foregone conclusion on what the solution must solve. The same drivers and goals for one organization may result in totally different responses than for another organization

Although buildings, apparatus and processes are part of the enterprise, it is the people who play a specific role to support business and to generate business. It is this human factor that to a large extent determines the response to the perceived business drivers and how best to go about realizing the business goals. And because each person or group of persons is accountable for one or more aspects of the business, they will have different interests in the response to the perceived business drivers and business goals. This is what is known as a *separation of concerns*, one of the cornerstones of IT architecture. Different people, different concerns; or better: different stakeholders, different concerns.

Stakeholders and Views

In this chapter we look at how IT architecture needs to perform a balancing act by listening to these stakeholders, discovering their concerns, and coming to a consensus among stakeholders to decide on the best way forward to realize the business goals. That is, we want to set up an IT architecture that provides a solution that fits all stakeholders. This will be done with some give and take from all sides, but at least with a mutual understanding and consensus about the way forward. Note that finding stakeholders and consensus is not by itself democratic or even honest. It is very much dependent on the organization, its culture, and the distribution of power.

Stakeholders

There are different influences that shape the final solution. Most important are the primary stakeholders who need a solution to satisfy their needs. The stakeholders for the solution to be architected are roughly all persons that have a vested interest in the final solution. A stakeholder is defined in ITSA as:

> Stakeholders are client representatives who:
> - Have the greatest impact on the project's success
> - Will be most affected by the project's results

They will be part of the process that defines the solution architecture. The primary stakeholders have formulated the organization's business goals, and therefore influence the solution that must support these goals, their job, their position, and the organization affected by the operational solution.

Equally, external factors, such as regulatory rules and legislation imposed on the client, influence the final solution. Privacy laws and accountability rules are examples of these external factors. These influences are not optional – they are mandatory.

Finally, the third category of stakeholders is the group that will use the solution as part of their job. These stakeholders will not define business goals, but they are part of the operational processes of the organization that wants to achieve these business goals. They may exercise some influence on the final solution, mostly in the area of ensuring that the solution fits in the best way possible into existing practices, processes, and existing systems.

This process, as depicted in Figure 10, seems simple enough. But how do we identify stakeholders and rank their importance, because no one is ever

Stakeholders

equal? Many studies have covered what is known as *stakeholder analysis*, which resulted in many academic and practical models in the management discipline. Stakeholder analysis aims to identify the individuals or groups in an organization that have an interest in the solution – either directly or indirectly.

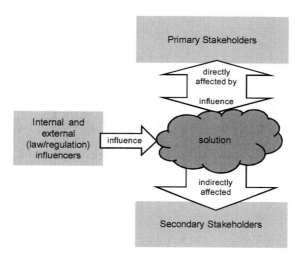

Figure 10: Stakeholder types

A search on the Internet for stakeholder analysis returns quite a few approaches each with its own merit.[28] [29] [30] One way to look at stakeholder classification is by attributes such as:

- Power (high, medium or low)
- Influence (either: supportive/positive, neutral or threat/negative)
- Interest, urgency for need of a solution (high, medium or low)

A good selection and participation of key stakeholders (a mix of primary and or secondary stakeholders) increases the likelihood of an architected solution that fits the organization. However, this fit cannot always be

---

[28] Mitchell, R. K., B. R. Agle, and D.J. Wood. (1997). Toward a Theory of Stakeholder Identification and Salience: Defining the principle of Who and What really Counts. *Academy of Management Review 22(4): 853 - 888*.

[29] Savage, Nix, Whitehead and Blair. (1991). Strategies for assessing and managing organizational stakeholders. *Academy of Management Executive 5(2): 61 – 75*.

[30] The project management hut (search for 'stakeholder analysis'), *Retrieved 2008 from* http://www.pmhut.com

Stakeholders and Views

guaranteed. If conditions among stakeholders cannot be met, the sponsor is preserved from unnecessary spending already. A potential project then does not start. We see here that architecture also functions as an instrument to identify, mitigate, or analyze risk.

The classification technique often used for the selection of stakeholders is the power-interest grid devised by Imperial College in London.[31] It is clear that stakeholders:

- With both power and interest are the ones to fully engage in the architecture and the subsequent solution.

- With power but limited interest can be employed to have major issues (that will grab their interest) settled.

- With low power but high interest are the ones to involve getting details settled within the larger picture that is defined by the powerful.

- With low power and limited interest are people to keep informed and on the supportive side, but one should not waste too much time on them.

Figure 11 illustrates these different types of stakeholders classified by their power and interest.

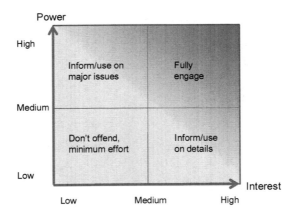

Figure 11: Power-interest grid

The selection of stakeholders is of paramount importance, only if we choose the right stakeholders a fitting solution can be architected. It is the

---

[31] Template document: http://www3.imperial.ac.uk/pls/portallive/docs/1/7339774.DOC

distinct role of the architect to guide this selection and sometimes deliberate creating force fields in architecture endeavors. This can be beneficial to solve the *unspoken* issues, create a solution that fits, and get the right 'DNA' (the right mix of stakeholders and their influence) to start a project. Stakeholders are important for the success of the architecture and beyond, but are most important in the early stages to ensure that the right direction is set – to a large degree set by their direct or indirect interest. The question remains: how do we find the right stakeholders and classify them? This is where the concept of views comes in.

Views in ITSA

Stakeholders have different interests, different concerns. This separation of concerns leads to different ways one can look at the problems imposed by the business drivers and possible solutions suggested by the business goals. Architecture addresses the issue of different concerns by defining different *views* to the problem and its possible solutions. Identifying the views immediately suggests the type of stakeholders to look for (see Figure 12). And once found, to rank them according to their influence, power, and interest.

The ITSA framework uses four views and, to prevent that architecture downgrades to a mere labeling exercise, it maintains a dependency between all four of the views. This ensures a seamless chain of justification of architectural elements – nothing is there without a reason – that results in a complete and consistent architecture:

- **Business view** – the problem and solutions seen from the business perspective: what business services do we provide to customers (fulfilling the business goals)

- **Functional view** – the solutions seen from a user's perspective: what functionality does the solution provide to its users to assist in their support to the business

- **Technical view** – the solutions seen from a constructor's perspective: what components are used in what configuration to enable the functionality, and how they are put together

- **Implementation view** – the solutions seen from a builder's perspective: with what means do we build the solution components, put them together and enable their use

Stakeholders and Views

 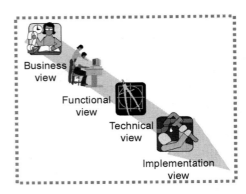

Figure 12: Stakeholders and views

Although Figure 12 may suggest that the views are handled in a specific waterfall order, where one view feeds into the next view, this is only true by first approximation. We always start with trying to address business related issues and concerns of business view stakeholders and work our way down through the views; the focus gradually shifts from what's desirable (business) to what's doable (implementation). During that journey, important issues may be raised in the current view that require a revisit of an earlier view where this was either overlooked or underdeveloped.

This heuristic approach makes sure the architecture is consistent throughout all views, addresses all issues relevant to the stakeholders, and crafts a solution that addresses the very essential aspects of the problem at hand. None of the architectural elements in any view stand on their own – they are all linked together to make sense and have an essential reason for being there. This is where ITSA uniquely differs from many other architecture methodologies. Many architecture methods also use the concept of views, but leave out any interdependencies among the views. This is a serious problem, as the chances are high that these methods result in weakly defined architecture elements without coherency.

Stakeholders of Views

Since the views represent separation of concerns, it is clear that various stakeholders provide the majority of input for the different views. As an example, Table 3 lists some generic job titles of people who have an important vested interest to shape the IT architecture and the solutions based on it.

The Four Views Revisited

Table 3: Views and their typical stakeholders

View	Stakeholders
Business	Business officers and managers, solution acquirer, business analyst, etc.
Functional	Solution users, business process designers, information modelers, etc.
Technical	Solution developers, technology consultants, subsystem suppliers, etc.
Implementation	Project managers, solution developers, solution testers, solution deployers, users/business managers, operators/managers, etc.

Based on stakeholder analysis, their input and contribution to the final architecture is rated and added. The typical questions that these stakeholders of various views may need to answer are related to the four traditional (IT management) aspects of any IT solution:

- **Agility** – issues on adaptability, flexibility, quick response to required changes

- **Quality of service** – issues on robustness, reliability, availability, ease of use

- **Cost** – mean and lean versus feature-rich in relation to (essential) value-for-money

- **Risk** – issues on 'good is good enough' or covering for all circumstances

The final architecture will contain all four views and the elements within them: principles, models, and standards. Before we discuss these elements further, we will revisit the four views in some more detail.

The Four Views Revisited

As a memory aid, each of the views and the sort of concerns stated in these views can be summarized by a single interrogative pronoun that captures the essence of the view, as illustrated in Figure 13. This helps in formulating questions on topics that the stakeholders in these views need to address:

- **Why** – Business view. Answers and choices based on the reason of existence of the organization and the reasons why things need to change: why are we doing this?

- **What** – Functional view. Answers and decisions based on what the solution needs to deliver to the users (all users, not only those using a desktop computer). End-user, GUI, (human) input/output focused: what must the solution do?

Stakeholders and Views

- **How** – Technical view. Answers and decisions on how the solution is composed and built up. Composition, IT infrastructure focused: how will the solution work?

- **With what** (or wherewith) – Implementation view. Answers and decisions on with what kind of 'matter' and processes the solution is realized. Typically involves products, project management, roll-out, and governance.

The coverage of each view may be extensive: many topics on which decisions and directions are needed. Prioritization may then be essential to focus on the most important ones first. These so-called topic areas are discussed in Chapter 9.

Figure 13: Views and their main concerns

Business View: The Why

Although formally not part of any view, the business drivers and business goals we discussed earlier are considered the starting point for the development of the business view's architectural elements. They have an impact on all views, however.

In the business view, the stakeholders (business officers and managers, solution acquirer, business analyst, etc.) indicate the direction in which the stated business goals are best achieved by implementation of new solutions or revision of existing ones. This view focuses on the business context of the

The Four Views Revisited

goals. The choices in this view are about the way the company wants to continue or change the way it conducts its business – through its services, processes, and type of customers, profit, partnering, value chain and others. And *why* those choices help achieve the business goals and relieve the business-stated driver stated pain, opportunity, or directive.

Functional View: The What

In the functional view, the stakeholders (solution users, business process designers, information modelers, etc.) indicate what functions are needed in order to support the change in conducting business, as formulated in the business view. Any decision made in this view must be grounded in statements made in the business view, or directly support the business goals. The decisions in the functional view are solution user related. What information or service does the user need to use or provide? In what ways is it presented? What business rules are executed, and what do they imply? What types of users are there, and what are their roles and responsibilities (and associated security clearances)? What other systems provide information we depend on, or depend on us? This view focuses on solution functionality, as well as some overall solution attributes (such as availability and robustness), not how the solution is technically structured.

Technical View: The How

In the technical view, the choices made must be related to the ones made in the functional view or business view. They must support the functionality needed and/or change of business stated in those views. This ensures that only those decisions are made that contribute to the business goals. The decisions in the technical view are very much solution or system structure related. What components, libraries, frameworks are used? How do they relate and communicate? How reliable do they need to be? And how about scalability, distribution packages, infrastructure? Note that in this view the focus is on construction techniques and the related technical components of the solution, not on specific brands or products.

Implementation View: The With What or Wherewith

Implementation view choices are rooted in business goals or choices made in any of the earlier views. Stakeholders for the implementation view focus on building the solution defined in earlier views. With what means is this achieved? The focus is on benefit realization, partnerships, and project organization including change handling, testing, and prioritization of delivery, roll-out methods, and possibly product selection if that is relevant.

The Focus of Views

As indicated earlier, the heuristic approach of architecture work means that the ITSA views are not processed in a strictly waterfall fashion. Although the chain of justification is top-down, the creative process requires us to add or consider choices we have made earlier in a particular view. For that reason, each view establishes more constraints on the solution. Starting from the desirable in the business view, we consider in each of the subsequent views how far we can make the solution realistically fit the needs of the stakeholders while at the same time serving the desirable business need. We 'narrow down' the solution towards the end of the chain of justification by making additional essential choices.

The implementation view is slightly different here. Many of the 'with-what' or 'wherewith' choices relate more to non-functional issues and choices that are made in the business view. After all, the implementation aspects of the solution have a more intimate (but not exclusive) relation to business choices and priorities than to functional and technical choices. For example implementation choices that depend on the business desire to continue operations while implementing the solution.

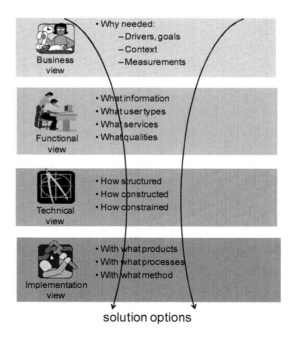

Figure 14: Narrowing down of solution choices

View Dependencies on Business Type

To emphasize this effect due to the heuristic approach, it is helpful to show the four views not in sequential order (as in Figure 13 and Figure 14) but in a more circular fashion as in Figure 15.

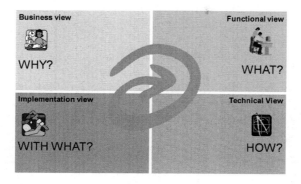

Figure 15: Circular influence among views

View Dependencies on Business Type

The stakeholders are key in defining what areas of concern need to be covered and where specific choices need to be made (to be discussed later in the chapters on topic areas and principles). Stakeholders in organizations that use IT as an enabler or as an empowering component have different interests and objectives than those organizations where IT is the main business, such an outsourcing organization. In fact, one can differentiate among four types of organizations:

- Organizations that use IT as enabling component and have their own IT division

- Organizations that use IT as enabling component, but outsource the IT to focus on their core business (named *outsourcing organization* in the remainder of this text)

- Organizations that have IT as their core business (we call this the *IT services* or cloud computing organization)

- Organizations that have IT as their core business but outsource part or all of it.

As we saw in the chapter on business drivers and goals, the business focus of the first two types differs from those of the last two types. But all must define a solution architecture that fits their needs and capabilities. The organization that holds all of its IT in-house uses the four views to determine choices on the desirable (business/functional) versus the doable (technical/implementation).

Organizations that outsource part or all of their IT still face the four views in IT architecture and also needs to make choices on the desirable and doable. However, some of the aspects are no longer the concern of the organization and are moved toward an IT Services organization. In order for both organizations to work together effectively, each must develop its own solution through architecture. The input to both architectures is different because the stakeholders and the business drivers and goals are different. We will provide a first impression of these two different architectures and the potential contents of the views in the remainder of this section.

The organization that outsources its whole IT needs to give careful thought about the complexity of the service management agreements made with the IT services organization.[32] Any agreement, usually a service level agreement, must be considered in relation to the business processes and other existing (service level) agreements; they need to be consistent and in support of each other. Such an organization also needs to determine what services it will consume and how these will be invoiced in a transparent way to the consumers. Internally, it needs to be clear on who pays for what services, or whether some overall payback or subsidy system exists. Because of regulatory obligations of an organization, it is often important to define how it can access the operational data and systems of the IT Services in order to verify and audit the level of compliancy by which the IT Services adheres to regulatory obligations. For example, if the outsourcing organization has commitments on privacy laws, it must impose these commitments on the organization that provides the IT Services. The outsourcing organization remains the prime responsible party, regardless of the fact that it outsourced its IT (see for example ISO/IEC20000). Figure 16 shows some of the concerns the outsourcing organization may have (left hand column). These aspects are mostly related to the functional view of the solution architecture.

The IT services organization will have to focus on providing the IT services and to provide information about the consumption of those services such that invoices can be sent. The types of services and their pricing depend on choices made on running their business – elements of the business view. How those services are best provided is determined in the technical view. The entire governance of the IT services is part of the implementation view,

---

[32] For example, simply stating that it will be ITIL compliant is not enough. ITIL is just a best practice that needs to be tailored to the client organization. It is also important to define who will structure the ITIL processes and which processes are relevant and need to be implemented.

Conclusion

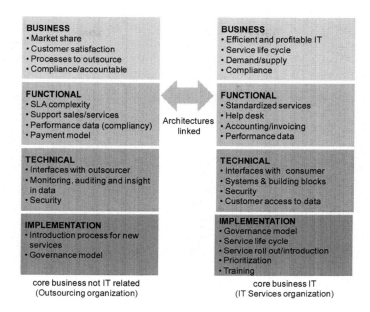

Figure 16 Topics in IT centric and non-IT centric organizations

which can include service lifecycle management aspects as defined in ITIL. The right hand column of Figure 16 shows this as architecture views and concerns for the IT Services organization.

The solution architecture of each of the two organizations, the one that outsources its IT and the one that sources it, will interact most strongly at the functional view level. This is where the 'What are we able to do?' question of the one is answered by the 'What do we provide?' of the other. Figure 16 represents the extreme case. In practice various levels of outsourcing are possible, from basic infrastructure components all the way up to complete IT business process outsourcing, shifting the focus and degree of interaction between the two solution architectures.

Conclusion

IT solutions are directly affected by primary stakeholders in the organization. The stakeholders represent their vested interest in the four views of ITSA: the business view, functional view, technical view, and implementation view. Each view has its own primary stakeholders, which by nature have very different interests. Architecture must carefully balance these interests and create consensus among the stakeholders about the essential characteristics of the IT solution solving the business problem. Choosing the right stakeholders is driven by factors of power, influence, and interest. Their

Stakeholders and Views

interest also varies depending on the type of solution that we are defining, which greatly depends on the core business of the enterprise. IT solutions for organizations where IT is the core business have different subjects to explore than organizations where the role of IT is to support a non-IT business.

7. Architectural Principles

> *Those are my principles, and if you don't like them… well, I have others.*
> ~*Groucho Marx*

> *Important principles may and must be inflexible.*
> ~*Abraham Lincoln*

The essential choices about a solution are documented as architectural principles. Principles allow us to defer the detailed decisions needed in realization projects so that we can concentrate on the key choices needed to solve a business problem. In ITSA, principles are set up in such a way that all choices are tied back to the business, and result in a seamless chain of justification. It allows no irrelevancies; all choices are there for a reason. Business drivers and goals guide the heuristic process to create consensus among all stakeholders that results in a coherent set of principles in the four ITSA views. Principles are powerful, as they defer unnecessary decision but simultaneously induce actions in projects.

In the previous chapters we introduced the ITSA framework with its concept of views. Views solve the issue of separation of concern. Although hinted at in the earlier discussions, the question that arises when one attempts to set up an architecture is 'How to present the properties of a 'system' in an abstract way, such that the follow-on implementation process (which includes design and development) has the necessary room to create a solution with the state of the art?' The ITSA framework defines architectural elements that accommodate this: principles, models, and standards. In this chapter, we take a closer look at principles.

Principles give us a way to both describe the characteristics of a solution without too much detail and guide the decision-making that is needed in the follow-on realization (design, build, and implement) process. A principle must lead to many correct decisions made on the path from architecture to final implementation. Principles are found in all of the four views and perform an important role within the IT architecture. Together with views (discussed in Chapter 6), they are the cornerstones of the concept of architecture.

Architectural Principles

The Purpose of Principles

The stakeholders in each of the views develop principles that express and record the essential choices they made. These principles describe the desired future state of the operational solution the stakeholders seek to define, and provide essential constraints for the implementation (design and construction) decisions. These choices are pivotal to the solution envisioned and must be made before any solution can be designed and implemented. The contents of these principles are about non-trivial matters. The 'art' of architecture lies in gaining consensus among the various stakeholders about these non-trivial matters, about which the stakeholders initially will have different opinions and may disagree. The architecture process will lead to consensus amongst them.

The essential choices are guided by the business goals and business drivers that led to the architecture initiative but also by the organizational culture, the stakeholders involved, and the environment and context within which the organization operates. It is important to stress, that business goals and drivers are the fundamental root of all principles. Every choice made along the way must ultimately support the business goals and resolve the issues of the business drivers. Principles matter! They express non-trivial choices where stakeholders may initially disagree.

All these factors result in a unique set of choices, documented in principles, for a specific organization. Any other organization facing the same business challenges may, and likely will, end up with a different set of principles that describe *their* unique desired future state because their influencing factors will have different values and content. It is extremely dangerous for an organization to simply adopt an existing architecture with all its principles or to have a consulting party define an architecture for them because neither has the insight knowledge of the organizations characteristics and may suggest IT investments that are not aligned with the organization's business. It is therefore fair to say that it is not possible to write a book with universally valid principles because the principles for a solution are shaped by factors in the business context that are unique for a given situation. This also positions any reference architecture one may come across for a particular IT domain. Such reference architectures are necessarily incomplete and serve as a starting point to develop a proper solution architecture that fits the organization. In moving from reference architecture to specifically a solution architecture, the reference architecture refers to issues that the stakeholders of the organization must come to agreement on. The documented principles reflect the choices made. Two organizations therefore may develop different solution architectures based on the same reference architecture.

The usage and meaning of the word principle is many-sided in our languages. Principles seem important to human behavior; for example Giddens,[33] a well known social scientist, explains principles as 'the most deeply embedded structural properties implicated in the reproduction of societal totalities'. Another usage of the word principle is, that it provides us a structure and a decision framework of essential truths, fundamental beliefs by which we agree to act. The many quotes about principles either reinforce their importance (as Abraham Lincoln does) or try to ridicule them (as Groucho Marx does), but in doing so acknowledge their importance. Webster's Dictionary defines a principle as:

> 1 a: a comprehensive and fundamental law, doctrine, or assumption
>   b: (1): a rule or code of conduct
>   (2): habitual devotion to right principles <a man of principle>
>   c: the laws or facts of nature underlying the working of an artificial device
> 2: a primary source: ORIGIN
> 3: a: an underlying faculty or endowment <such principles of human nature as greed and curiosity>
>   b: an ingredient (as a chemical) that exhibits or imparts a characteristic quality
> - in principle : with respect to fundamentals <prepared to accept the proposition in principle>

The meaning and usage of principles in IT architecture follow almost all of the above definitions. This emphasizes their importance.

Range and Reach of Principles

The content of architectural principles is predominantly motivated by three dimensions:

- **People** – roles, jobs, and responsibilities may be different in the new situation.
- **Process** – how things are done and organized as part of the solution.
- **Technology** – addressing information related techniques and technologies.

---

[33] Giddens, A (2008), *The Constitution of Society*, Polity Press, Cambridge.

Architectural Principles

Principles for a well-architected solution address all three dimensions to some extent. A solution architecture that only contains principles addressing the technology dimensions ignores the other two, is likely to be incomplete, and will fail to deliver. For example, IT solutions that ignore the process or the organizational dimension will very likely fail to deliver. The same is true for any other architecture that leaves out one of the other dimensions.

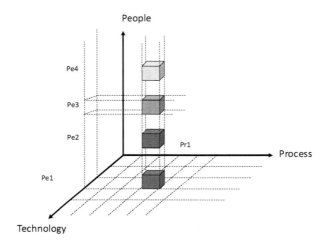

Figure 17: The solution and its principles in the architecture space

This concept is illustrated in Figure 17. Each combination of choices for people, process, and technology result in a solution *space*. Four of these possible solution spaces are illustrated in the figure. Only one solution space will contain the essential elements to define the architecture that represents a solution that fits the perceived problem. Only this solution space matches the specific context and specific choices made by the stakeholders in the dimensions of people, process, and technology. This underlines our statement that a different architecture for the same organization will likely solve a different problem.

The illustration also answers the question 'When is architecture necessary?' Architecture is necessary when essential choices still need to be made. For example, when the entire IT landscape is a given (the point along the technology axis is fixed); there are still people and process issues (along the other two axes) that need to be sorted out. Once all essential choices are made and known in all three dimensions, and thus we can identify a specific point on each of the three axes, the solution space is known. Architecture creates coherency among the three dimensions.

The Power of Principles

The number of principles that must be defined in order to determine all essential characteristics of a solution will be limited. Depending on the scope of the architecture, a few dozen in number is typical. Defining principles is very much bound by the overall motto 'everything you need, nothing you don't.' The emphasis is on the effectiveness of principles instead on their number, so they must be strong in guidance and direction as well as long lasting and effective in the follow-on design process.

Principles invite many decisions that are to be made in the follow-on realization process. These decisions are best left to the subject matter experts. For example, if a principle states that a web portal is used to support a business goal, it is irrelevant whether the portal is based on Apache open source or Microsoft's IIS (Internet Information Services), or what it looks like. It is best left to the design phase for users and the IT developer community, and who have the detailed knowledge and experience to make the appropriate decisions. The architecture states the presence of a web portal – prohibiting users from designing a client-server application or anything non-web portal. Design and construction decisions must not conflict with the principles defined in the architecture. This will ensure that decisions at this level will not favor a local best or cheap situation that is detrimental for the corporate level business goals the architecture aims to support.

In the realization process, the principle stands and guides. In other words, it is not up for debate. This is nicely summed up by Boar in his book on enterprise architecture (see call-out).[34]

> Principles provide enduring overall direction and guidance for the long term evolution of IT assets. They provide a basis for dispersed but integrated decision making, and serve as a tiebreaker in settling disputes.
>
> Principles address the perpetual management problem of influence at a distance. Though the decision maker cannot be everywhere, and neither can nor should make every decision, agreed-to-principles provide influence without presence. This is very important if one hopes to promote coordinated but independent actions across a large and often opinionated organizational community over time.
>
> ~Bernard Boar

---

[34] Boar, B.H. (1999), *Constructing Blueprints for Enterprise IT Architectures*, John Wiley & Sons Inc, New York.

Architectural Principles

If a situation does occur in which the realization process cannot live up to the principle, the architecture should be revisited by the architect and the appropriate stakeholders. This is the concept of *architecture governance*, which we will discuss later.

Principles in ITSA

Principles are found in each of the four views defined in the ITSA framework. As such, we find principles in the four cells of the ITSA framework, as illustrated in Figure 18. By nature, principles are very text oriented as they document essential choices. Their more visual counterpart, the architectural model, is discussed in Chapter 10.

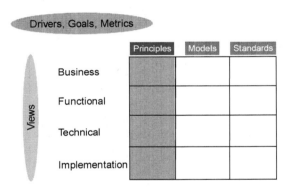

Figure 18: Principles in the ITSA framework

The definition of a principle in ITSA is described as:

> A fundamental approach, belief, or means for achieving a goal. It is timeless – it is how the system is meant to work

Principles are important directives for the follow-on design process so as to support the business goals for which the architecture is defined. For this reason, it is not possible in ITSA to accept principles that do not directly or indirectly (via support of other principles) support the business goals. This explicit linking of principles to support business goals is a rather unique feature of the ITSA framework. This seamless chain of justification imposes important attributes for the principle, and is formatted in a standardized structure in ITSA. These attributes, *Statement, Rationale, Implications, and Obstacles* are all part of the formatted structure of the ITSA principle and are described in Table 4. In the next sections, we will visit each of these

Principles in ITSA

attributes in more detail. It is important to notice that a principle refers to the *entire* structure: including its statement (called 'principle' for simplicity, as in the graphic in Table 4), rationale, implications, and obstacles.

Principle Statement

The principle statement describes a desired property of the solution as if the solution exists today. Principles are forward looking and therefore stated in the present tense, and they should be true when the solution is realized.

Table 4: The structure of a principle

Principle identification	<B/F/T/I>Pnn
Principle statement	Short description of the principle, describing the desired future state.
Rationale	Link to related principles (in any higher view) or business goals that support this principle. Additional supportive statements like best practices can also be added but cannot be the only reasons.
Implications	Conditions of making this principle happen. The principle will affect a number of areas that must be defined such that they comply with the principle. This may result in the need for some additional principles in views farther downstream. Implications are necessary to realize and within our reach to effect. They result in a list of actions to do. We know we can do them; we just have to do them.
Obstacles	Potential or actual situations that may prevent the principle from being realized. They are things we do not have full control over, but can identify and try to risk-manage. They result in a list of actions to mitigate risks.
Actions	Actions are not officially part of a principle, but result from the principle's implications and obstacles. They are assigned to an individual or a function and have a deadline by which the action must be completed. Where implications and obstacles are consequences of the principle's future state, actions have a shorter time span to be realized. Actions in ITSA can have a many to many relation with principles

Note that the statement needs not be true today and, more often than not, will not be true. But it describes how the situation will be once realized. Architecture principles therefore describe the vision of this future state and describe it in a way as if that future state were true today. For example, picture the following situation:

- Today each sales channel has its own ordering process (business driver: this is inefficient and costly – the derived business goal is to become efficient and cost-effective).

Architectural Principles

- The future final state has all sales channels funnel into one ordering process (principle) to realize the business goal.

To make the principle strong and compelling, it is important to state the principle in the present tense without any 'would,' 'should,' 'could,' 'might,' or 'ought to' hopeful statements. The architecture tells us how it is going to be and the principles describe the new situation. No uncertainty here! Therefore, we must not state:

> 'All sales channels should funnel into the same ordering process.'

but

> 'All sales channels funnel into the same ordering process.'

Obviously this could raise a question about how one needs to handle exceptions to these principles. There are no exceptions. The above principle is firm and clear; it does not allow any exceptions. It is powerful choice and doesn't allow people to find ways around it because it fits their own agenda better. If there are situations that do need to include exceptions to the principles, it should be clearly outlined in the principle itself. As an example, consider the following principle:

> 'All sales channels funnel into the same ordering process. Exceptions are permitted only by formal approval process.'

The addition of an approval process will lead to a principle implication that requires this process to be defined and formally accepted. This way it is still clear when, and when not, exceptions are permitted. Such a process will become an architectural standard (to be discussed in Chapter 11).

Principle statements have no ill-defined elements, nor do they have vague or political multi-interpretable words as 'where appropriate,' 'mostly,' 'when possible,' and such. These vague situations must be clearly defined and listed as implication and result in standards. Additions like 'when possible' then becomes 'always except for predefined cases.' The standard, another architectural element in ITSA, serves to list predefined cases. Of course, the standard should not inherit the 'when possible' political exit doors either! We will discuss the ITSA standard in a later chapter.

Rationale

ITSA has principles for each of the four views; they are very specific for that view, and they are interrelated to the other views. As said before, principles

Principles in ITSA

are there for a reason and therefore must support the business goals for which the architecture is defined. This support can be done directly by referring to one or more business goals, or indirectly by referring to another principle from a previous view. This guarantees that, for example, a principle in the technical view supports a principle in the business view, which in turn supports a business goal. To refer back to principles and goals in the ITSA framework, we use the rationale attribute of the principle structure.

In some cases, the definition of a principle may be more powerful if an additional attribute is added as a rationale: consequences of not obeying the principle. This may be an additional source of information to the people who design solutions that comply with the architecture. These people, or designers, are made aware not only of the reasons why the principle choice is made, but also the penalty of not following it. Additional rationales can also include best practices. Figure 19 illustrates the seamless chain of justification between principles. For clarity, only the rationales connecting adjacent views are shown – but remember that any connection to any previous view is also allowed.

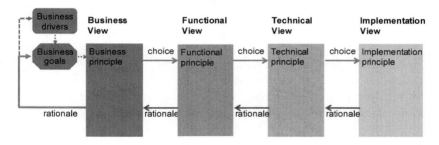

Figure 19: Link between principles of views

Implications

The principle statement describes a desired future state as if it were true today. As a result, changes in the current situation need to happen before the principles can be realized; these are changes that are in reach and control of the current architecture. In ITSA, the attribute of the principle that contains these necessary conditions is called an implication.

Implications are necessary conditions to realize the desired future state. All of these conditions are met in that future state and together they enable the principle to be true in that future. This is a good checkpoint when developing principles and their implications. Given all implications realized in the future, will this make the principle come true too? If not, there are additional implications we need to specify.

Architectural Principles

Implication of principles serve two purposes: a) they provide conditions to be met before a principle can become true and b) they provide a forward linking to the next view as they motivate the formulation of one or more follow-on principles. As with the principle itself, they have dimensions of people, process, and technology.

Because implications are unavoidable consequences and necessary consequences for the principle to become true, actions may be needed to realize the implication hence the supporting principle. Actions that follow from implications are a good source for a project manager's work breakdown structure when the architecture is implemented.

Please note that Implications are consequences of the principle – not additional choices that are not intrinsic properties of the principle statement. This would lead to a principle-within-principle situation that would destroy the chain of justification; this sneak in of additional definitions without proper linkage to the business goals and/or principles must be avoided at all times. After all, implications have no rationale themselves the way principles do to ensure proper goal-means linking. The example (see call-out) on mass public transport is an existing everyday situation and demonstrates how implications are meant to work.

Obstacles

Obstacles are issues that may prevent the principle from coming true. In contrast to implications, obstacles are not fully under the control of the realization project. However, we do acknowledge that they exist and try to limit the impact the obstacle may have, by proper risk mitigation through actions.

Examples of situations that are not (fully) under control are external regulations imposed on the organization (e.g. US Food and Drug Administration (FDA) rules, Sarbanes-Oxley or Basel II compliance) as well as customer behavior (we cannot force people to buy our product, but we can entice them with promotions, loyalty programs, etc.).

In practice, the number of obstacles is much smaller than the number of implications. Those obstacles that remain require actions to manage or mitigate the identified risks. As such, obstacles will provide input to any project manager's risk plans.

Principles in ITSA

Architecting Mass Public Transport

Assume we architect mass public transport within a city. The business principle 'We only use a bus-system for inner-city mass transportation' motivates a functional principle: 'Travelers can only (dis)embark at defined points along the route, known as "bus stations" or "hubs".'

What implications does this functional principle have? How do we realize bus stations? Some possible implications are:

- Locations for stations have been selected along bus routes (Actions: Determine bus routes, set up criteria for station locations)
- Bus stations accommodate expected route demand and transportation equipment ('buses') (the main function of a bus station) (Actions: Determine demand on routes, estimate number of buses at stations at any one time.)
- Bus stations are equipped to handle handicapped travelers (tells us bus stations are for all travelers) (Actions: Determine what types of handicaps can be dealt with, personnel training for this, personnel availability.)
- Bus stations are instantly recognizable to travelers by building style and logos (this identifies to travelers whether they see a bus station) (Actions: Determine building style and logos.)
- Traveler and bus movements are strictly separated for maximum safety (further detail on the main function of a bus station) (Actions: Separate bus lanes from corridors on station layout. Ensure access to bus only via platform entrance, travelers areas needed away from bus lanes)

Improper implications would be:

- Bus stations have ticket selling facilities. (Explanation: This is another choice – tickets may also be sold on the net, by the driver, in vending machines: a principle on ways of payment. Tickets are not an intrinsic property of a bus station)
- One type of bus is used (to standardize bus lanes). (Explanation: Selecting buses is not part of the station functionality).
- Petrol and gas fill-up facilities are present at bus stations (Explanation: It is another choice. Do all stations have those? What about terminal stations and en-route gas stations and other stations?).

Actions

Both implications and obstacles will result in a number of activities to be performed to realize the implications (and hence part of its principle) or to reduce the risks identified by the obstacles. Actions are specific tasks to be

Architectural Principles

performed and have a due-date and an individual accountable for the execution of the action. Actions are derived from implications and obstacles, but are themselves not an attribute (or part) of the principle. Because of their different nature, actions are subdivided into actions resulting from implications and actions resulting from obstacles. An example structure of an action is shown in Table 5.

Table 5: Example action structure

Action	
Action description	
Implication/Obstacle	
Who	(action 'owner' and support)
When	(to be started and/or completed)
Estimated effort	
Dependencies	
Deliverable	

The World of Principles

In the previous section, we discussed the attributes of a single principle. Principles in different architectural views have a connection with each other through the goal-means hierarchy of the rationale attribute. This was briefly mentioned in the section on rationales. Figure 20 shows a more detailed version of the relation among principles compared to Figure 19.

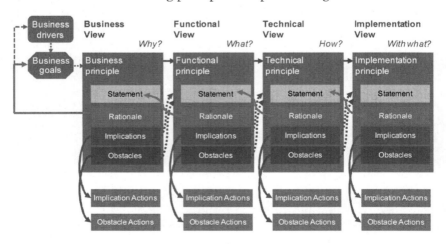

Figure 20: ITSA goal-means hierarchy of principles

The World of Principles

Some comments about Figure 20:

- To keep the picture from becoming too convoluted, only the rationale links are shown that link a principle to another principle in an earlier view. Remember, however, that for example an implementation principle may have a rationale pointing to a technical principle (as shown), but may equally well link directly to a functional or business view principle, or a business goal if this is appropriate.

- Implications and obstacles of any principle may be cause to define additional principles in follow-on views. Those additional principles will have a rationale pointing back to the principle with the implications or obstacles that motivated it. Note that this is not compulsory: follow-on views may have principles that do not originate from the previous view principles. A view may be skipped, or a principle may directly support a business goal or business driver (the dotted arrows forward obey the same logic as the backward-linked rationale arrows).

- Implications and obstacles result in different types of actions.

The linked goal-means hierarchy allows the architect to do some simple but effective completeness and sanity checking on the obtained set of business goals, business drivers, and principles in all four views.

To perform some of the bookkeeping tasks, it can be helpful to use automated tools such as simple databases, spreadsheets, or sophisticated architect workbenches. By inspecting the principle-rationale links, they can inform us:

- Do all principles have valid rationales (i.e. other principles or business goals or drivers)?

- Do all business goals have principles to support them (i.e. is none overlooked)?

- Do all principles (in)directly support business goals and drivers (i.e. no orphans)?

- How strongly are the business goals and drivers supported by (multiple) principles?

In addition, such a tool can assist in some 'what-if' impact analyses by following the links between principles defined in their rationale attributes:`

- Which principles need to be revisited when a business goal is no longer valid or is modified?
- Which principles are to be realized first if goals are prioritized?
- What consequences does the change or removal of a principle have on the business goal(s) it supports, and how does it affect principles further downstream that support and rely on this principle?

Principles Differ from Goals

People often seem to have difficulty separating business goals from (business) principles. We mentioned this in the chapter on business drivers and goals. A business goal is something the business wants to achieve, *regardless of the way how* (as long as it is legal and ethical). It is the answer to the (repeatedly) asked question 'Why do we want this?' Because of the many ways available, it is the principle that gives guidance on the (best fitting) manner by which the goal is reached – the principle contains that choice. Some examples:

- 'Increase revenue by 10% in the next year' is a goal.
- 'Increase revenue by 10% by employing a web channel' is a mixture of a rationale (the goal 'Increase revenue by 10%') and principle choice ('We employ a web channel').
- 'Market share is increased by using web channels' is similarly a mixture of a goal ('market share increase') a principle ('by using web channels') and an assumption.

From the above we can state the distinct differences between principles and (business) goals as follows:

- A goal is something we want to achieve, and mostly plays a role in the business case for which the architecture is set up.
- A principle is a (fundamental) *means for achieving* a goal.
- Multiple principles may be needed to fully accomplish a goal.
- A single principle may support several goals.
- Upstream principles also become the rationale for lower-level principles. This is because principles may have complex implications

that warrant the need of one or more downstream principles to achieve it.

- In ITSA, only top-level goals are given the name 'business goals.' So, a principle is simultaneously:
    o A means for accomplishing a business goal or supporting the case of an upstream principle.
    o Representing a set of one or more implications (rationales), which are addressed by downstream principles.

Principles Differ from Requirements

We dedicate a separate chapter (Chapter 12) to architectural requirements because principles and requirement have very different purposes in the concept of architecture – hence a principle is not a requirement and vice versa. Principles are choices, a fundamental means to achieve a goal. Choices made in a context, giving strategic direction. Requirements are concrete instantiations of principles at the operational level. A principle is more observational (e.g. 'is,' 'has') in guiding decisions allowing various choices for implementing it, whereas the requirement is more active, dictating. Requirements therefore often have the word 'must' as part of their phrases, but principles never have.

In practice, requirements may exist before principles (and the architecture) do exist. These requirements often come from disjointed sources and their validity and consistency with the desired business goals and drivers must be checked. Therefore, the architect must challenge each requirement by asking for the related principle. This should consistently link all those principles into the architecture framework. The principles and/or requirements that do not fit in this structure need to be reconsidered and, in the worst case some of the principles and/or requirements must go. This is illustrated in Figure 21.

From the consistent ITSA framework, its principles will give reason for requirements to be defined. These will partly be the same as the initial ones, but more likely new ones or modified ones will emerge. But now they all support the one architectural view of the solution ahead.

Architectural Principles

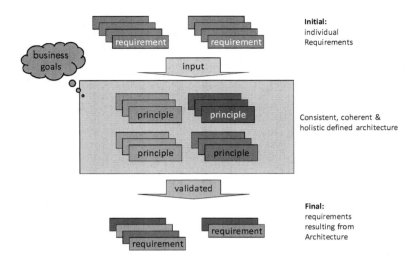

Figure 21: Coherent requirements result from architecture

Principles Differ from Policies

Some organizations have *policies* in place and consider them to be principles. As long as this is just a different use of words, the architect should accommodate this. However, a policy is something very different from a principle. Webster's Dictionary defines a policy as:

> a: prudence or wisdom in the management of affairs
> b: management or procedure based primarily on material interest
>
> a: a definite course or method of action selected from among alternatives and in light of given conditions to guide and determine present and future decisions
> b: a high-level overall plan embracing the general goals and acceptable procedures especially of a governmental body

Policies are about definite *procedures* and *plans* to respond to certain affairs or situations. Principles also cover affairs and situations but in a more general context. They are less definite, as they cover a wider range of possibilities. Policies prescribe a particular action given that specific criteria A, B, and C apply. Principles give guidance and direction under these criteria but also apply to (slightly) different situations than criteria A, B, and C define. Policies can be implemented in rule-based systems. In a deterministic manner, a policy comes into effect. Principles are never caught in a rule-based system. They can, however, serve as the basis for several policies.

Conclusion

We have seen that a principle is one of the architectural elements that define the properties of a solution. They help us to postpone the decisions that concern the level of detail designers and builders typically need so that we can focus on the essential choices necessary to find a solution that fits its purpose. Principles are guided by business drivers and goals, they represent the consensus among stakeholders, and they are defined in each of the four ITSA views. We are unlikely to see exactly the same principles in various architectures, as each architecture addresses a unique problem; different architectures solve different problems. The structure of the principles in ITSA is such that they build a seamless chain of justification. Through the rationale, everything is tied back to the business goals and drivers and ensures that nothing is defined without a reason. The implication and obstacles list the necessary conditions and problems to solve in order to make the principle happen. Principles are a powerful instrument as, through actions, they create motional energy in projects, but principles also help us to scrutinize the usage of requirements.

8. Effective Principles

> *If you use these principles wisely and intelligently, there can be no uncertainty as to the outcome of any endeavor, and no limit to your possibilities.*
>
> ~Roger McDonald

A successful architecture greatly depends on the formulation of its principles. Only effective and coherent principles can result in an unambiguous architecture that fits its purpose and drives change. Besides that principles must fit the solution, they also must fit the organizational culture. For example, some organizations do reward risks, some just don't. The 'art' of defining good principles is about crafting principles that are unambiguous, unique, strong and long lasting, have the right justification, and result in the desired effects.

Some say that defining good principles is an art. It demonstrates the mastership of the architect if they are durable and really address the heart of the matter. In his book *The Timeless Way of Building*, the well-known (physical) architect Christopher Alexander states:

> 'Let us start with a very commonsense example. Suppose you are at a place. We have a general sense of that something is "right" there; something is working; something feels good; and we want to identify this "something" concretely so that we can share it with someone else, and use it over and over again. What do we have to do? As we will now see, there are always three essential things we must identify. What, exactly, is this something? Why, exactly, is this something helping to make the place alive? And when, or where, exactly, will this pattern work?'[35]

This vision on what enables building patterns comes very close to what we mean by the essentials of architectural principles.

The previous chapter discussed the structure of an architectural principle and the important role it plays in the IT architecture for the desired solution. In this chapter we provide techniques to formulate strong principles that are

---

[35] Alexander C, (1979), *The Timeless Way Of Building (p. 249)*, New York: Oxford University Press.

Effective Principles

effective and constrain the follow-on realization processes. The following topics are covered in subsequent sections:

- The decision content of the principle
- The independence or orthogonality of principles within the same view
- The authority of guidance of a principle
- The linking of principles to business goals or upstream principles
- The type and content of implications of a principle
- The type and content of obstacles of a principle

Principle Statement: Content

The effectiveness of a principle depends on the context in which it is used. Except for weak formulation, there is no such thing as a right or wrong principle. It all depends on the situation and the context of the organization that formulates the principle. Reference architectures contain token principles, often with candidate implications and rationales. These are to be taken as starting points for developing the principles fitting to the organization with choices made by the organization's stakeholders. They are never to be copied and adopted as-is unless the stakeholders have reached consensus about such a principle.

To formulate principles that are effective for a particular situation or organization, it is helpful to view the various solution domains as a spectrum between two extremes. Figure 22 illustrates this for a couple of domains (Information, Risk, Technology, Development, and Organization) that can be typical for the stakeholders.

Figure 22: Spectrum for various principle topics

Principle Statement: Content

Table 6 shows some possible principle statements that reflect both extremes of the spectrum of possibilities. These principles can be part of existing reference architectures; the organization must decide whether they apply to their situation and, if so, what would be the most fitting description (between the two opposing extremes).

Table 6: Example principles in the spectrum of various domains

Domain	Principle	Opposing principle
Information	Information is made available to and shared between internal parties. Exceptions only after formal approval of Information Board	Information is classified and accessibility is restricted on basis of user category
Risk	IT is business empowering	IT is business enabling
Technology	We select leading edge IT components to open up new markets	IT components have a proven market presence, maturity and stability
Development	All IT services are outsourced	The organization owns and controls all IT services and development thereof
Organization	IT decisions are taken on a business or operational unit level	IT decisions are made at enterprise level

A choice like 'Information is made available to and shared between internal parties' is just as valid as 'Information is classified and accessibility is restricted.' But both choices are not likely to apply within the same organization or context; more likely, they represent two extremes in a spectrum of possibilities for information sharing. At a governmental organization such as a Ministry of Defense, 'accessibility is restricted' may be more suitable, while the sharing attitude may apply more to the educational and research world of universities. For commercial companies, an effective principle may fall somewhere between the two extremes.

For any specific architecture, a particular principle statement may be somewhere on the scale from 0% to 100% on the spectrum. It never states the obvious, as that would not allow many follow-on decisions to be based on it. This also provides a useful sanity check for any principle. Given a choice that is proposed as a principle, one may consider whether someone might create an argument against it. If that argument can be defused by using the reasons why the principle was stated as is, the principle represents a choice that is made for valid reasons. If we cannot think of an opposing statement for that principle, we should consider whether the proposed principle represents a specific choice within the spectrum of two extremes or is a simple truth or trivial statement, and therefore should be removed as principle.

Effective Principles

Principle Independence: Orthogonality

Strong principles are also independent of one another in their content (but support and reinforce one another between views through their rationale). In mathematics, one would say they are orthogonal. In database normalization, one would say there is no redundant information in principles. This has an impact on the following three situations:

- A principle statement contains parts of other principle statements: remove it.
- A principle statement is a composition of other principle statements: it replaces those others.
- A principle statement is only partly unique and contains partly the same content as some other principle statements: make the unique part a separate principle.

Principle Statement Contains Parts of Other Principle Statements

Any principle that can be identified as being a composite of (various parts of) other principles must be removed because it adds no new essentiality and restates what has already been stated: it is about architectural essentials. An example is given in Figure 23, where the four shown principles might have the following values:

Principle 1:	'We favor COTS solutions.'[36]
Principle 2:	'Exceptions to architecture only through approval process based on business case.'
Principle 3:	'We only deploy stable technologies, proven in the field.'
Principle 4:	'We buy proven technology before we make. Exceptions only on a proven business case.'

Here the principle 4 has already been stated as part of the other three principles and, as such, adds no value:

- 'We buy before we make' is similar to principle 1.
- 'Proven technology' is covered in principle 3 (but at the same time is also more extensive).
- 'Exceptions' are covered in principle 2 (is also more extensive).

---

[36] Commercial, off-the-shelf (COTS) is a term defining technology which is ready-made and available.

Principle Independence: Orthogonality

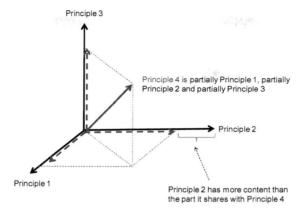

Figure 23: Principles must not decompose into composite principles

Principle Statement Is Composed of Other Principle Statements

The second situation is a special case of the previous one, but with a radically different outcome. The principle statement represents the complete content of one or more other principle statements. This means the principle is the sum of the other principle statements. With the ITSA mantra 'everything you need, nothing you don't,' this one principle can replace the others.

In Figure 24 we see that the three superfluous principles exactly add up to the new principle 4 that is to replace them, whereas in Figure 23 the principles along the axes have more content than the part they share with the superfluous principle 4, which does not add anything unique.

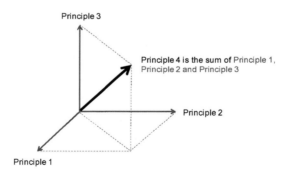

Figure 24: Individual principles that sum up must be combined

Effective Principles

A Principle Statement Is Only Partly Unique

In the third situation, some principles share a common element. Consider making this common element a separate principle and rephrasing all principles in such a way that they are mutually orthogonal. This is shown in Figure 25, where the potential principle 2 includes part of what an existing principle 1 also states. As an example:

> Principle 1: 'Exceptions to architecture only through approval process based on business case.'

This principle is partly repeated in proposed principle 2 that reads:

> Principle 2: 'We buy before we make. Exceptions only on a proven business case.'

By removing this duplication, we're left with 'We buy before we make,' which we can keep as is or reformulate to become the new principle 3:

> Principle 3 'We favor COTS solutions.'

These final two principles are orthogonal to one another. In real life, of course, there can be multiple principles involved instead of only two, as in this example. This will also complicate matters for the architect to detect such situations and rectify them. But every effort must be taken to develop a proper set of independent principles – 'everything you need, nothing you don't.'

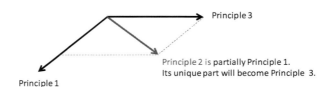

Figure 25: Independent principles by removing commonalities

Principle Guidance: Authority

Principles must be firm, strong, and long lasting. Once established, they are not up for debate, and they provide direction and are the basis for follow-on decision making. Therefore, principle statements must be firm and without

Principle Linking: Rationale

doubt or unintended escape clauses. The following guidelines may help as a checklist or 'litmus test:'

- Principles are stated in the present tense – they describe a (future) desirable state as if it were true now.
- Principles have no 'should,' 'would,' 'could,' 'whenever,' 'where appropriate,' and other types of weak elements. They are clear and unambiguous.
- Principles are normally not true today (unless they describe a situation that is true today but requires effort to keep it true – for example to stay compliant with government regulations).
- Principles are compelling and likely to generate many right decisions, as they cover a wide range of situations (unlike policies or requirements).

Principle Linking: Rationale

Each principle must have a valid reference to one or more business goals, drivers, or principles in earlier views that it supports. The support must be significant and substantial. Additional rationales are allowed, including mention of best practices and consequences to the organization by not following the principle, but at least one significant link to earlier view principles or business drivers or goals must be present. Without this linkage, as summarized in Table 7, the principle is not supporting the IT Architecture and its solution.

Table 7: Possible linkages of rationales

References Belongs to	Business goal	Business principle	Functional principle	Technical principle
Business principle	✓	–	–	–
Functional principle	✓	✓	–	–
Technical principle	✓	✓	✓	–
Implementation principle	✓	✓	✓	✓

Implications: Conditions on Principle-described State

Implications are necessary conditions of the future state described by the principle. As such, we can ask ourselves the following questions regarding implications:

- Do all implications together make the future state described by the principle statement true?
- Do implications take into account the people, process, and technology aspects?
- Are implications stated as conditions instead of 'to do' lists – which should then become actions?
- Do implications relate to the future state described by the principle statement? Are they related to the principle statement? In other words, is someone trying to sneak in an irrelevant principle that breaks the chain of justification?
- Are actions (with owner and due-date) associated with implications?

Obstacles: Issues on the Principle Beyond Our Control

Many of the questions asked for implications can be asked for obstacles as well, but some are specific to obstacles with regard to the aspect of 'not being completely under the control of the realization project.' The principle's obstacles and implications are not two sides of the same coin. If an obstacle can be rephrased to be an implication, then it should become an implication. For example, 'We do not have the expertise' is not always an obstacle. Often it can and should be rephrased as 'Expertise is hired externally.' This, in fact, turns the obstacle into an implication and becomes under our control. The same is also true for the inevitable 'There is no budget.' Perhaps the budget is not available as one lump sum, but a phased or prioritized approach might release the needed funding in several rounds. Obstacles that can be inversely rephrased as implications must be changed into implications. Some issues to consider when formulating obstacles:

- Can the obstacle be rephrased as an implication (i.e. is it really beyond our control)?
- Do obstacles take into account the people, process and technology aspects?
- Are (risk-mitigating) actions (with owner and due-date) associated with obstacles?

Conclusion

It takes some effort to create effective principles. Effective principles are needed to make the architecture successful. To some degree, effective principles can be found in organizational culture (for example, the reluctance or reward of risks). But also, the way principles are formulated has an impact on the effectiveness of principles. The 'art' of defining good principles is about crafting principles that are unambiguous, unique, strong and long lasting, have the right justification, and result in the desired effects.

9. Topic Areas

> *With over 75 questions to choose from and only 60 minutes available, it came down to choosing questions that covered major issues.*
>
> ~Chad Dotson, Attorney Wise County, Virginia

To solve the right problem, it is necessary to have a good understanding of the areas of concern in which architectural principles need to be defined. Knowing these so called topic areas already is a first step in the right direction if they have a strong relation to business drivers and goals, and their content is not clear-cut. Topic areas are where the scope of the architecture is set and stakeholders have their vested interest. In fact, this is where architecture becomes specific and domain expertise comes into play. For example, topic areas needed for application architecture will differ from infrastructure architecture topic areas.

With the introduction of views and principles, we made the first step toward looking at solutions from different angles and describing them at an abstract level that is sufficient for the follow-on implementation project. We could question whether the views provide enough differentiation to define principles for a complex solution. We introduced the people, process, and technology dimensions earlier, but these can be still too broad to give us a grip on complex problems.

To address all of the aspects a solution needs, such that it also solves the *right* problem, the architecture process would benefit from a good understanding of the areas where principles need to be defined before we actually begin to define principles. In fact, these areas define the scope of the solution and its architecture. This helps us to focus on the essential parts of the solution and not overdo the contents of the solution or, even worse, create a solution that does not solve the problem at all. In short, creating a solution that *fits* – 'everything you need, nothing you don't,' as the mantra goes.

In ITSA, we use the term *topic areas* to refer to the areas in the views where principles, models, and standards are defined. The versatility and holistic approach of ITSA prevents any formalism in names and content of topic areas; this is typically where domains of interest manifest themselves. Stated differently, architectures related to, for example, outsourcing or applications have different topic areas. In this chapter, we explain how to identify suitable topic areas, how they can relate to each other, what their characteristics are, and how they relate to stakeholders.

Focus on Essentials: Topic Areas

To develop an architecture that addresses the stated business drivers and goals can be a large endeavor. Defining topic areas effectively breaks up, or scopes, the total architecture and the problem it needs to solve, into a set of manageable pieces. These are pieces that are considered relevant by the different stakeholders, that need attention, and that need choices.

Topic areas are used in all four ITSA views. Within each view, there are multiple (topic) areas of interest, potentially each of interest to a (partially) different set of stakeholders. In order to focus on the essential areas, we must decide which areas to focus on first to obtain the boundaries of a first draft architecture. Topic areas that qualify as important meet the following criteria:

- They are strongly related to business drivers and goals.
- Their content is not clear-cut: choices in that area (formulated in principles, models, and standards) are needed to mold the architecture and obtain consensus amongst stakeholders.
- They are important to the stakeholders and do matter.

This means that, out of the many areas of the architecture that can be thought of for the business view, only the important few are selected to inspire the first cut on the architecture. These are illustrated in Figure 26 by the filled rectangles in the business view – a subset of all the areas makes up the business view plane in which stakeholders are interested.

Topic areas are ideal vehicles to create an initial architecture. The results will provide sufficient evidence to determine whether the future solution makes sense and is within the capabilities of the organization, or whether it requires the organization to reconsider or do some soul-searching before going for the entire solution. The same applies to all other views. The selected topic areas are all directly and indirectly related to the business drivers and goals – the context of the problem.

If topic areas are related to upper stream topic areas, they are likely to contain principles linked to upper stream principles through their rationale.

How to Identify Suitable Topic Areas

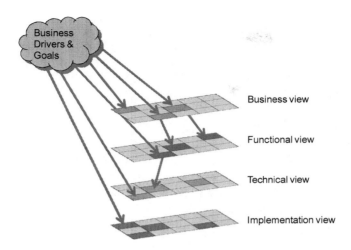

Figure 26: Topic areas in different views

As an example, Figure 26 illustrates this for two topic areas in the business view, which lead to topic areas in the lower stream functional view.

How to Identify Suitable Topic Areas

For many people, the process of identifying topic areas for the first draft of the architecture seems to be cloaked in mystery. Indeed, there is no mechanical process to determine what topic areas to use. However, it should not be an 'art' or 'miracle' to define proper topic areas for each ITSA view: they must be essential areas for which principles are needed in any one of the views. How can we determine these topic areas?

In practice, topic areas present themselves in a very natural way while setting up taxonomies for the problem. Useful sources for topic areas are, for example, the Balanced Score Card and process or service definitions. This is where previous knowledge and familiarity with similar problems is important, either from our own experience or by re-using reference architectures that address similar type problems (if available). The important topic areas are those that their stakeholders felt important, and where principles are needed.

The Problem Taxonomy

Taxonomies can be set up in various ways. The first taxonomies by Linnaeus were applied to life forms: animals and plants.[37] What is important? Their

---

[37] Carl Linnaeus is often called the Father of Taxonomy. His system for naming, ranking, and classifying organisms is still in wide use today.

Topic Areas

size? Number of feet? Way of locomotion? Their habitat? Their shape or color? Linnaeus structured taxonomies in such a way that life forms could be identified and catalogued. That would solve his problem of creating order in the chaos of life forms. Had Linnaeus been a chef, he might have come up with quite another taxonomy more fitting to classify and order aspects of taste and meal preparation time.

Clearly there is no taxonomy that fits all situations. Depending on what we intend to use the taxonomy for, some taxonomies are preferable to others. This is also true for topic areas. Once our client problem is identified as set of business drivers and goals, we look for topic areas as taxonomies for this problem, taking into account the people, process, and IT technology situation of the client. Questions that help in structuring the taxonomy and therefore identifying the topic areas fall into three categories:

- **People oriented** – What part of the problem is people related? What aspects of the organization, roles, education, and lines of authority are contributing to the problem or not helping to solve it, and or where do they not address some of the organization's (future) needs?

- **Process oriented** – What part of the problem is process related? What sort of processes seem to be missing (are desired), duplicate effort, block future efforts and are considered in the way of progress, are processes in need of revision? Do processes make logical chains? What are the contents of a process? What best practices exist in that industry? What about the business-supporting primary processes and the administrative- or IT-supporting processes?

- **IT Technology oriented** – What part of the problem is IT related? What landscape of applications exists, what do they support, is there overlap, do they map to processes, who owns the information chains? What information objects or stores exist? What is their life cycle? What problems does the current IT landscape pose to its users and what is its contribution to the business?

The taxonomy of people, process, and technology is the same as used in the implications of principles. It will come as no surprise that a process-type topic area (such as *life cycle* in Figure 27), may trigger principles that strongly support the process dimension choices. We may also encounter identically or similarly named topic areas in two or all of the three branches of people, process, and technology respectively – in which case the principles that originate from those topic areas will have implications in all these three areas of people, process, and technology.

How to Identify Suitable Topic Areas

The Stakeholder View

ITSA identifies four different views, with four different sets of stakeholders, as explained earlier in Chapter 6. The topic areas identified based on the problem taxonomies now need to make sense to the stakeholder. Part of the sense-making is implicit in the problem statement, but we need to verify with the stakeholders of the various views whether the identified topic areas are indeed areas of concern, where a clear direction is needed for solving the problem.

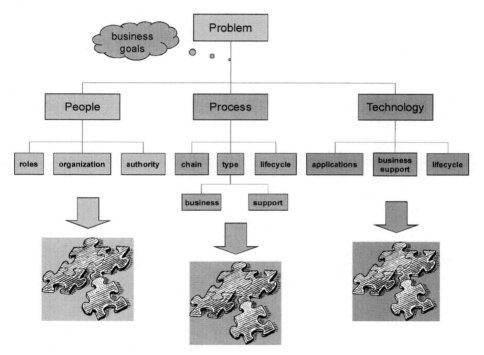

Figure 27: From initial problem statement to topic areas

Only the client stakeholders can confirm topic areas, as they know the organization's context, its politics, its culture, and its internal workings. They may agree with some of the topic areas we, as the architect, identified, but they may be triggered to propose others that they feel are important. In doing so, they may partly modify the problem taxonomy, but this is fine because the architecture and its direction ultimately need to be supported and enforced by the stakeholders.

Characteristics of Topic Areas

Effective Topic Areas

An effective topic area focuses on the essential, important areas of the solution. They will elicit the architectural elements: principles, models, and standards. Therefore:

- Each topic area represents an aspect of the enterprise where the architecture is going to change decision-making and behavior. They must be related to business drivers and goals. They help in grouping principles and models to be defined for these areas.

- Different views may or may not have the same topic areas (and if they do, they will be handled differently – in accordance with the view).

- Topic areas should be small in number (to be manageable) and agreed to by the client.

Once we have defined a set of topic areas, we need to ask our self 'What principles will be defined for these areas?' Ultimately, that is what topic areas are supposed to do: invite the client to make choices in these areas. If you cannot think of any principles, the client may not be able to do so either.

Lifecycle of Topic Areas

Topic areas come into play when we need to scope the architecture. Within its scope, the architectural elements are developed and defined. Once the topic areas have served their purpose, they fade away and are no longer seen or used. They are instrumental in focusing attention on important and essential areas in which we define architectural principles and models. Once this is achieved, the topic areas serve no further purpose. They are not architectural artifacts themselves, and they are therefore no longer used.

Example Topic Areas

Because each problem is different, and for each problem there is a best fitting solution for a particular organization, it may be clear that there is not a fixed set of topic areas. There is no 'one set fits all.' At best, there are known reference architectures that address (part of) the problem and hence provide a head start by suggesting topic areas. Many problems have recurring themes too, so a likely list of potential topic areas can be set up as a reference – a source of inspiration. The final list of topic areas is the one that is agreed

Example Topic Areas

with the main sponsor of the architecture endeavor. The examples listed here are potential candidates, but are by no means the only ones possible.

Business View Topic Areas

Topic Area	Subjects for principles
Market Place	Growth, diversification, globalization
	Customers, partners, suppliers, channels, distributors, agents
	People and organizations; the nature of the (new) relationships
Value chain	Products and services, processes/flows, information
	Resources, front-end/back-end entities, business functions, Balanced Score Card
	The primary business entities that affect and are affected by the solution
Business environment	Industry/domain structure, competition, legal
	Other business entities and conditions that affect/are affected by the solution

Functional View Topic Areas

Topic Area	Subjects for principles
Users/roles	End user types, 'system' user types, organizations, responsibility for content
Services	Input, output, dependencies, portfolio, service levels
Information	Information maintained by the system, externally visible data
Applications/system functions	What the system does; includes use cases and visible system behavior
Operational processes	System management, content preparation
System attributes	Accuracy, scalability, performance, availability, security/privacy, maintainability, evolvability
Interfaces & integration	Human and system interfaces, points of contact, integration required
Related systems	Information exchanges with other systems that interact with this system

Technical View Topic Areas

Topic Area	Subjects for principles
System structure (static)	Subsystems and components, data model, interfaces
System operation (dynamic)	Timing/control flow, data flow
Infrastructure	Applications, middleware, platforms, networks, storage
System attributes	Resilience, scalability, etc.
Environments and tools	Runtime, development/test, deployment, management; includes runtime libraries, application frameworks, development languages, test suites, software distribution mechanisms, system management frameworks, etc.

Implementation View Topic Areas

Topic Area	Subjects for principles
Products	Mapping of logical components to specific products (or product criteria)
People/organization	For the program/project, and/or post implementation
Processes	Change management, planning, design, development, deployment, operation, maintenance
Rollout/plans	Rollout priorities and methods; includes resource, time, and cost estimates for above processes
Configuration	Version management, parameterization, mapping of logical components to physical locations
Management of Change	IT governance, decision making, culture

Conclusion

Topic areas divide the problem we face into smaller pieces, and they also help us to set the scope of the architecture. They are instrumental in focusing on important and essential areas where architectural elements like principles, models, and standards are needed. Every view is populated through the aid of topic areas. Topic areas most likely differ from view to view, but not always. Some views can have similar or identical topic areas. After principles, models, and standards are defined, topic areas do not serve a purpose any longer in the architecture process except as a very logical or natural division of the matter at hand. With topic areas, an architecture becomes specific in the sense that it illustrates the solution domain the architecture is targeted for (for example an outsourcing solution, an infrastructure solution, etc.).

10. Architectural Models

We do not imitate, but are the model to others.

~Pericles

Models can make or break architecture. A bad model can introduce ambiguity. A good model provides insight and direction in an essential part of the architecture. Architectural models are connected to principles and effectively reflect the choices denoted by the principles. Models also highlight the way principles interact with each other and are very effective for managing complexity. Good architectural models follow rules to accomplish their purpose. A model and a picture are not the same thing!

The definition of relevant principles is a main ingredient of the IT architecture. It is a very heuristic process and is very text oriented, as we have seen in the previous chapters. But words can only clarify so much. They are instrumental in describing many situations but fall short in situations where visualization is more appropriate. The visual counterpart of the principle is the model, and a model is just as decisive and directive as a principle. One might say that a model is the twin brother of the principle, with equal power.

In contrast with principles, models are very visually oriented and fill the architectural description where 'a picture says more than a thousand words.' But models are not pictures! Broadly stated, any architectural choice made that is not in the form of a principle, is in the form of an architectural model. A model highlights the way some principles interact with each other or reveals additional principles. Where it reveals new principles, these should best be made explicit by adding such a principle to the list of existing principles. Models are very effective for managing complexity by focusing on the essential elements and aspects and thereby enabling the communication and decision making process.

Architectural Models

What Is a Model?

Let us start with a common definition of 'model' as it is understood in general. A dictionary is a good place to find such definition. Webster's Dictionary defines a model as:

> 1: structural design <a home on the model of an old farmhouse>
>
> 2: a usually miniature representation of something; also : a pattern of something to be made
>
> 3: an example for imitation or emulation
>
> 4: a type or design of product (as a car)
>
> 5: a description or analogy used to help visualize something (as an atom) that cannot be directly observed
>
> 6: a system of postulates, data, and inferences presented as a mathematical description of an entity or state of affairs

An architectural model conforms to this definition and has one or more of the following characteristics (using the list numbers of the dictionary entry):

1. It shows the structure and coherence of aspects of the solution and reveals the implicit assumptions and choices made with this structure.

2. It is a visualization of an important part of the solution, such as a graphical user interface (GUI) or layered composition. The model is not a copy of the end solution, as it focuses on an important part. As Kühne strikingly states:

   > 'If I build a car according to an original being precise in every minute detail, I have not constructed a model but a copy. If I use the copy in a crash test, I have not performed a model simulation but a real test run. Copies neither offer the advantages of models (typically cost reduction) nor their disadvantages (being incomplete, only containing the essentials).' [38]

3. It is a pattern to be copied and implemented in the solution. It can be used on its own without knowledge of the 'entire solution.'

---

[38] Kühne, T (2004), What is a model?, In Jean B´ezivin and Reiko Heckel, editors, *Language Engineering for model-Driven Software Development*, volume 04101 of *Dagstuhl Seminar Proceedings*, 2004.

4. It shows the 'outside' of the solution – usually GUI or report based, but may also show organizational aspects.
5. It is an abstraction of (part of) the solution: showing the parts that matter and are responsible for shaping the solution: the principles behind it.
6. It makes predictions through calculations (by spreadsheet or program) to show the behavior of the solution under different conditions (bottleneck finding, stress simulation, process flow, capacity planning).

From the above, it can be deduced that a model is not limited to a *picture* of some sort: spreadsheets and other representations also apply. In practice, we often see a *picture* incorrectly presented as an architectural *model*. But without the rules that apply to a model, it simply remains what it is: a *picture*. The rules and requirements that apply to a model are discussed later. We must first have a look at when it is appropriate to apply models.

When to Use Models?

Models enable the communication and decision making process. Therefore, models are not useful in the following situations:

- The problem as well as its response is well known: no choices needed. Apply best practices. In fact, in this situation, architecture itself is not needed as we are dealing with well known territory where all major choices have already been embedded in the available best practices.
- The problem is relatively small and modeling would be overkill. Never follow a method that describes modeling without first considering whether it adds value.

This automatically presents situations where modeling is useful:

- The problem is complex or not well understood; alternatives must be evaluated, choices are needed.
- Communication is required with and between many stakeholder members.
- The originators of the model will not always be present during the solution development, yet their choices must be complied with.

Architectural Models

This should sound familiar, as the reasons for developing models are the same as for developing principles. Models are the principles' twin. This does result in the following consistent handling of models:

- Models show the effect of how existing principles work together or enforce one another.
- Models revealing new principles must lead to the explicit definition of these principles and the linking of them to the model.

Requirements for Architectural Models

What makes a model an architectural model? To promote a model into an architectural model, it needs to meet certain requirements, the same way principles do on the textual side of architecture. Many of the requirements are the same, but models have additional requirements that relate to their visual nature.

Models Have a Purpose and Focus on Essentials

First of all, a model must have a purpose. Like principles, models must support and be linked to the business goals – directly or indirectly. A principle represents and formulates a choice that is fitting for the architectural context and narrows down the spectrum of the follow-on implementation project. Similarly, a model represents and formulates a structural choice, with a well defined and consistent level of detail, to provide directive guidance on the way forward, as required by the IT architecture of which it is a part.

Just as a principle addresses the essentials of a particular aspect of the architected solution, so does the model. It visualizes the essential properties of some aspects of the solution. For each type of solution stakeholder, there are different essential aspects and therefore different models, but all represent the same issues, from different stakeholder perspectives. We can see this from the following comparison:

- A future house owner is interested in the floor plan and orientation of the house and much less in the way the walls and floors are reinforced (he will take those as a given). The builder is especially interested in the materials and reinforcements to use and not whether the house is oriented to the south for optimal daylight usage – he will take that as a given.
- A business stakeholder is interested in the business entities such as customer and invoice, and their relationship to the business process.

Requirements for Architectural Models

The IT stakeholder is interested in the definition of tables, rows, fields and indices that make up the customer and bill data and how to ensure its availability and speed of access.

All models are linked to each other and support the same set of business goals – the same way principles do.

Models Support the Business Goals

Second, an architectural model must have a rationale. Principles initially are just statements of choices. We could have made any other choice. But there is a specific reason, a rationale, why we made this choice instead of any other: because this choice is the one best fitting the goals addressed by the architecture. In the same way, a model has been selected above all other possible models because it fits the architecture best. The rationale of a model is based on business goals, principles, or other models.

Models Are Unambiguous

Third, a model must convey a unique message. Principles should be unambiguous and provide directive guidance from the architecture on the way forward. Models serve the same purpose. They, too, must not be open to interpretation. Everyone who looks at the model must interpret its (visual) directives in the same way.

In the engineering discipline, this is accomplished using formal notations with precise meaning that can be used repeatedly. The same is true in the software engineering levels of IT where, for example, UML or ERD diagram elements have precise meaning to all readers. [39] [40]

The IT architecture discipline is much less mature in this respect and presumed models often are casual, and have graphics chosen according to personal preference and with imprecise meaning. As Bernard Boar so strikingly states, 'the current and predominant individual approach to architecture diagramming makes purposeful architecture development, communication, adherence and evolution extraordinarily difficult, if not impossible.' [41] To avoid this problem, an architectural model lacking formal notation standards needs to include a precise legend that specifies what is what, and this legend must be consistent among different architectural

---

[39] Entity-Relation Diagrams – technique for database design.

[40] Unified Modeling Language – set of diagrams to describe a software system based on use cases.

[41] Boar B.H. (1999), *Constructing Blueprints for Enterprise IT Architectures*, John Wiley & Sons.

Architectural Models

models. It is worthwhile to make these legends a standard within the architecture, to ensure its use throughout the architectural models.

Models Have a Level of Abstraction

Fourth, a model must have a specific level of abstraction. Different models focus on essential aspects for different stakeholders, but within a single model there must be no mixture of conceptual, logical, functional, or physical elements. These are different levels of abstraction and often have different stakeholders (see Figure 28). A model must differentiate levels of abstraction in its representation:

- **Level 0** – represents the holistic essential aspect – a conceptual, high level model that may also be used to 'sell' the desired new state to the stakeholders who will fund the architecture initiative.

- **Level 1** – represents a more detailed view of part of the Level 0 at a logical level.

- **Level 2 and below** – are appropriate in the blueprinting phase of the architecture – they become more detailed and limited in scope.

Modeling should stop at the level where *enough is enough*. The recurring mantra in ITSA, 'everything you need and nothing you don't,' applies once again. Models convey choices regarding structure to the point where they support the proper execution of the architecture. Anything below this level is best left in the experienced hands, minds, and judgment of those who have to create the environment and systems directed by the architecture.

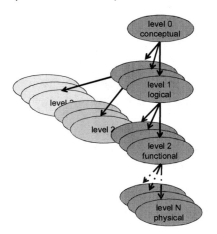

Figure 28: Models and their levels of abstraction

Models in ITSA

Within the framework of ITSA, models are the second ingredient in the architectural description. Models are the visual counterparts of principles, with the same decisive and directive power. The relationship among architectural models in ITSA (Figure 29) shows that they:

- Can be linked to other models in the same view (more detail) or in a view upstream (translation into view-specific aspects).
- Are linked to principles (where they visualize the interaction or mutual influence of principles on each other). Primarily, this will be to principles in the same view (which, in turn, will address principles and goals in other views upstream).
- Are directly or indirectly linked to the business goals that gave rise to the IT architecture.

The definition of an architectural model within ITSA is:

> An IT architectural model is a representation of the essential properties of some aspect(s) of a system

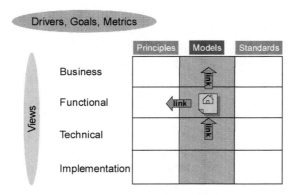

Figure 29: Models link to principles and other models

Unlike several other architecture methodologies, models are considered an essential part of the ITSA framework – on equal par with principles, and therefore are long lasting. This also implies that architects do not 'whip up another model' on the spur of the moment. They may do charcoal sketches and brain dumps while doodling on paper, whiteboard, Visio, or PowerPoint, but they are just that: a sketch, a picture. Of course, there is nothing wrong with these sketches when they are used as vehicles or discussion elements in the process of defining a proper model, but the follow-on realization project must be supplied with proper and coherent architectural models.

A Standard for Models

Given the requirements imposed on models and the need to be architectural (essential) by nature, it is good to standardize the documentation of a model. Table 8 shows the essential elements for documenting a model.

Table 8: Documenting models

Model ID:	<B/F/T/I>Mnn
Purpose:	Short description of what the model presents
Related to:	Link to related models and (existing or newly revealed) principles as well as additional best practices
Legend:	Definition of model elements (if needed)
Timeline:	Model of today, tomorrow, 5 years out, final state
Description:	Any further description that may be required. A lot of description indicates the model may need revision and is not self-explanatory and unambiguous.

Models by ITSA View

A number of more or less formal modeling techniques are available for each of the four views of ITSA, mostly based on de facto standards. Specific information on the purpose and meaning of each of these models can be found in reference books, and more recently, also on the Internet's Wikipedia online encyclopedia.

A novel way to present existing types of models is provided by Lengler and Eppler, who present model types in a periodic table. We know this structure from chemical elements with similar behavior when ordered in the same column of the table.[42] Lengler and Eppler tried to do something similar for modeling techniques, where the *elements* of models are clickable to reveal more detailed information. The classification is based on data, information, concepts, metaphors, strategies, and compound visualization.

The following list can serve as a checklist for using models in architecture endeavors:

---

[42] Lengler R., & Eppler M. (2007). Towards A Periodic Table of Visualization Methods for Management. *IASTED Proceedings of the Conference on Graphics and Visualization in Engineering (GVE 2007)*, Clearwater, Florida, USA. (http://www.visual-literacy.org/periodic_table/periodic_table.pdf) and www.visual-literacy.org for visual presentations.

Conclusion

- Does it have a single type of stakeholders as its target audience (such as business managers, CxO, end users, developers)?
- Does it have a single level of detail (no mix of business, conceptual, logical, functional, or physical elements) and a single purpose?
- Does it describe the current as-is, an intermediate, or the final future desired state?
- Are all elements used in the model uniquely defined and unambiguous for the target audience?

As a double check, we may present our model to a fellow architect on the project, and ask him or her to describe its purpose and see if the model is as unambiguous as we wanted it to be. All stakeholders should have the same interpretation; bad things can happen otherwise, as Ferguson states below.

> What's the number one 'programming tool' for business professionals? PowerPoint. If business professionals can use PowerPoint, I wonder whether we can nudge them into another tool to do business modeling. They already do business modeling, but they do it using documents that get handed to programmers. Programmers guess what the documents mean and bad things happen when programmers guess. I wonder whether we can do something cleverer. In business schools, they teach a discipline called structured English and various diagramming techniques. Maybe these could form the basis for programming business services.
>
> ~Dr. Donald Ferguson, Microsoft Architecture Journal 11

Conclusion

Models have their own special purpose in an architecture framework. They effectively reflect the choices revealed by principles and also highlight the relationships among principles, if a model reflects more than a single principle. Just as with principles, every view has models: business models, functional models, technical models, and implementation models. Effective models help us to understand complex architectural issues, but that requires us to follow some rules when we create models. Models in ITSA must have a purpose in the architecture (a sheer reason to be there), focus on essentials, and be limited to one level of abstraction. Ambiguity in models is a deadly sin, as stakeholders must be able to recognize their needs with a single interpretation.

11. Architectural Standards

> *Of course they are out of date. Standards are always out of date. That's what makes them standards.*
>
> ~Alan Bennett

Architectural standards constrain the choices available in the follow-on development activities in terms of uniformity in concepts, processes, technologies, protocols, and so forth. This ensures coherency with other IT solutions and predictability during the realization of the IT solution. Architectural standards are part of the ITSA architecture framework, and they serve as concrete ingredients to requirements that need to be defined.

Architectural standards are the third ingredient in ITSA's architecture framework, next to principles and models. Standards make the architecture real and relevant. IT organizations use architectural standards to create an agreed or corporate set of key data entities functions or technologies or processes – their names, their definition or descriptions.[43]

Standards prescribe how to accomplish something. This promotes uniformity and predictability during the process in which the architecture is realized through the realization project. In this regard, the ITSA framework is also a standard – specifying the way architectural principles and models are documented.

The Purpose of Standards

Like most words, *standard* may mean different things to different audiences. Webster's Dictionary defines a standard (as intended above) as:

> 1: something established by authority, custom, or general consent as a model or example: criterion <quite slow by today's standards>
>
> 2: something set up and established by authority as a rule for the measure of quantity, weight, extent, value, or quality

---

[43] Carbone, J.A., (2004), *IT Architecture Toolkit,* Prentice Hall Inc, Upper Saddle River NJ.

Architectural Standards

Common in both cases from the dictionary's definition is that an authority establishes standards. That authority for IT architecture is represented by the stakeholders or ultimately the architecture office. The standard is a rule for a measure – in IT architecture, mostly for the conduct of processes or structures.

While principles and models provide guidance and span a longer time, standards determine a specific choice within that guidance, and are directly obligatory in that respect. Future developments may leave the principle untarnished (for example: 'a single data exchange method is used') but may force or benefit from another choice for a standard (initially: 'data exchange is standardized through DCE,' later: 'through CORBA,' and currently: 'through web services'). Standards, therefore, tend to change more often than principles or models. They are the *configurable* aspects of a principle, but they ensure that all stakeholders make the same choice at any one point in time.

Standards in ITSA

Within ITSA, an IT architectural standard is defined as:

> A standard is a well-defined convention or measure with which a system must comply.

Standards are defined in each of the four views of the ITSA framework (see Figure 30). They directly relate to, and are the result of, implications in principles or models. Where a principle states a uniform way of working, mechanism, process, or other one-way-to-do-it mechanism, invariably one of the implications of such a principle is to define what this one-way-to-do-it comprises. The result of this effort is a standard, either one that already exists in the market and is adopted by many (de facto) or one that is formally controlled (de jure). A variation of the latter is any corporate maintained and exercised standard. The role of standards in IT architecture is as:

- An implementation decision of a principle
- A set of characteristics, conditions, constraints, measures, disciplines, or processes
- Used for constraining and/or evaluating the development, implementation, and management of a product or system

Standards versus Requirements

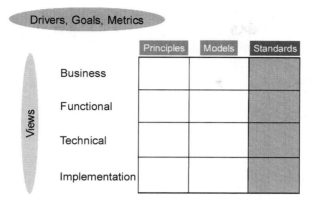

Figure 30: Standards in the ITSA framework

Standards make the architecture real and relevant. Because they are the result of implications of principles, they can also be subdivided in terms of:

- **People** (for example certification, or a utilization target like '70% utilization')
- **Process** (for example change control, project management (e.g. PRINCE II), problem management steps, SOPs (Standard Operating Procedures), or time restrictions such as 'Response time within 5 seconds')
- **Technology** (for example Operating Systems, protocols, or development languages such as 'C# as development language')

Standards are required to guide implementation projects in designing, building, and deploying IT related solutions.

There is no formal way in ITSA for describing a standard. In many cases, it suffices to reference *de jure* or *de facto* standards by their name or by the formal document in which they are described. Where a standard is specific to the architecture, a formal standards document is written, given a unique identification, published, and configuration-controlled.

Standards versus Requirements

Standards and requirements are often interchanged in loose talk, as are principles and requirements. Yet they are all different. In the chapter on principles, the difference between principles and requirements has already been discussed. Where do standards and requirements differ? Standards are an element of the IT architecture and, as such, where the related principles result in the formulation of requirements, the architecture standards are the concrete ingredients of those requirements. At times, standards and requirements may be identical in text, yet they perform different roles: standards specify how it is, requirements dictate a need. For example, where a principle asserts the use of one development platform, the standard resulting from the principle's implication may be to use the Java J2EE platform. This will then be a requirement for any proposal requested to implement the architecture.

Conclusion

An architectural standard is a necessary element in the ITSA architecture framework to further constrain the IT solution. In contrast to principles and models, which provide guidance in the follow-on realization project, standards are obligatory in the follow-on realization. We use standards to ensure coherency with other IT solutions. Notice that standards differ from requirements in the sense that standards define how things need to be done, while requirements dictate a need. Standards can already be existent in an organization, either de facto or de jure, but new standards can also be defined when we architect a solution.

12. Architectural Requirements

> *The very first requirement in a hospital is that it should do the sick no harm.*
>
> ~Florence Nightingale

Where principles provide the fundamental means to achieve a goal, architectural requirements ensure that the proposed solution really satisfies the business needs. Requirements confirm the nature and scope of the problem to be solved; without architectural requirements projects more than likely will deliver solutions that do not solve the problems we face. As with principles, architectural requirements are also essential by nature, meaning that they are architecturally significant. In other words, having listed many requirements, as seen very often in requests for proposals, does not necessarily help us to satisfy the business need or solve the problem. Architectural requirements are also used during solution acceptance from an architectural viewpoint: did the IT solution solve the business problem for which the architecture was defined?

ITSA is strongly principle-driven and, in that respect, is very different from traditional requirements engineering. With principles, we have a fundamental approach or means for achieving a goal, but we still need requirements to specify what it is the solution must satisfy. So, to define a solution that truly solves the problem we are facing, we need both architectural requirements and architectural principles. We will see that they are complementary to each other. They go hand in hand when we define architectural descriptions, but requirements serve a different purpose in architecture work than principles. As we mentioned before, the architecture process, by nature, is very heuristic. It is common practice that it starts with some first drafts, often done in workshops with stakeholder representation (architecture concept)[44] or in other less interactive engagements. At this stage, the first principles, models, and standards probably are not fully detailed and of a sound level of architectural quality – they are the first drafts. In fact, it is not uncommon that the first potential principles are phrased as requirements, which demonstrates the difficulty (in the architecture process)

---

[44] See Chapter 4 for the introduction of the architecture concept.

of eliciting the real essential issues that motivate the solution. Although the differences between principles and requirements are not subtle, in practice people do have difficulties understanding these differences. Gradually developing the initial sketches into a fully elaborated architecture blueprint typically involves reworking (better formulating) principles and testing their full validity with the stakeholders. This process also involves the formulation of requirements that specify completely and unambiguously what the solution must satisfy to solve the problem the business faces.

This chapter is not intended to be a how-to guide in engineering requirements. Its sole purpose is to explain how architectural requirements differ from architectural principles. It should provide a good understanding of the concept of architectural requirements and the role they play in architecture work, and lead to greater insight into the concept of architecture. We will see later that the difference between requirements and principles actually exposes one of the fundamental differences between architecture work and design work.

Why Architectural Requirements and What Are They?

Suppose we are asked to create a solution. The first and most pressing question we have is, 'What problem must the solution satisfy?' This is a very obvious question, because we need to know what the solution needs to do, such that it will in fact solve the problem! Usually the problem to be solved originates from a business goal which, along with principles, models, and standards, motivates the architectural requirements. These architectural requirements motivate use cases and architectural design elements. By 'architectural,' we mean anything that is architecturally significant, i.e. there is only one acceptable way for stakeholders to do it.

The purpose of architectural requirements (which we will refer to as requirements) is to confirm the nature and scope of the problem to be solved and ensure that nothing is missing in the proposed solution to satisfy the business needs. Without having requirements, we would be in the dark running a project, and more than likely we would deliver a solution that does not solve the business problem. Although the solution might be a good and working one, if it does not solve the business problem it is considered worthless by the business! Requirements serve three purposes:

- Confirmation of the nature and scope of the problem. (What is the problem?)
- Understanding of the capabilities of the solution. (What must it do?)

Why Architectural Requirements and What Are They?

- Acceptance of the solution when deployed. (Was the problem solved?)

To serve these three purposes, requirements need to specify what should be implemented to solve a problem. They describe how a system or solution should behave, or they describe system properties or attributes. They constrain the development process of the system or solution. If we depict the whole process from problem identification to solution as a V-shaped lifecycle, we see that requirements concern the acceptance of the solution. This is illustrated in Figure 31.

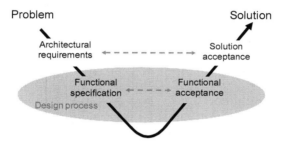

Figure 31: The V-lifecycle

We can think of requirements to be solution focused, as we can also see from the way Webster defines a requirement – addressing conditions for a necessity. Webster's Dictionary definition of a requirement:

> something required:
>
> a: something wanted or needed:
>
> necessity <production was not sufficient to satisfy military requirements>
>
> b: something essential to the existence or occurrence of something else: condition <failed to meet the school's requirements for graduation>

The way ITSA defines a requirement is very similar, although it does so from a solution point of view. The ITSA requirement definition:

> A property or capability of an architected solution, clearly derived from business goals and business, functional, technical, and implementation principles. Requirements specify completely and unambiguously what the solution to the problem must satisfy.

Architectural Requirements

Then What Are Project Requirements?

Requirements elicitation within ITSA concerns the solution only and is gleaned from the principles, models, and standards. The requirements also follow the four ITSA stakeholder views. Business requirements reflect business objectives (financial needs, innovation needs, etc.). Functional requirements explain all end user features of the system; they reflect what the solution actually needs to do. Technical requirements are those requirements not always directly associated with specific functionality (security, performance, etc.). Implementation requirements relate to the implementation of the solution (deployment order, data conversion, training, etc.).

In contrast to architectural requirements, *project* requirements are all those requirements that are internal to the project or assignment. What are the needs for a development environment (servers, storage, networking, etc.)? What are the needs for a testing environment? What development tools are needed? The architect does not control project requirements; likewise, the project manager does not control requirements that concern the architecture of the solution.

What Do Architectural Requirements Look Like?

The objective of specified requirements is a communicated shared understanding of what the solution must satisfy among all stakeholders. As with principles, requirements are expressed as written text in a natural language, supported by appropriate analysis models. Good requirements must be actionable, measurable, testable, related to identified business needs or opportunities, and defined to a level of detail sufficient for system design. See the structure in Table 9.

Table 9: Architectural requirement structure

Requirement ID:	\<B/F/T/I\>Rnn
Specification:	The requirement statement (narrative)
Justification:	Goal, principle, standard, etc. that the requirement addresses
Source:	Where requirement came from, who proposed it, document that identifies it, etc.
Impact:	Overall significance
Issues:	Actionable issues to be resolved
Related requirements:	Requirements that are have (inter) dependencies

How Do Requirements Differ from Principles?

We already explained that architectural requirements within ITSA follow the four stakeholder views. As with architectural principles, architectural requirements also can address different topic areas and subtopic areas.

How Do Requirements Differ from Principles?

Let us consider a best-case situation with solution requirements that are complete, concise, and correct, with a good formal presentation. This looks very promising to enable us to create a meaningful solution. However, this situation does assume that the stakeholders a) have a thorough understanding of the problem and b) fully understand the necessities of the solution to the problem. Therefore, interpretation differences can still exist among stakeholders and those involved in the realization project, and there is no guarantee that the solution will actually solve the problem!

The full depth and breadth of the problem in business (information) systems is rarely understood well, as they are complex and full of legacy, politics, etc. Fortunately, the ITSA framework with its chain of justified principles rooted in business goals provides us a rigorous goal-means analysis to fully understand the problem and define an appropriate solution for it.

With principles, we have a concept that provides the means of which things are intended to work in the future state. The designer can independently make decisions on how to construct the solution. As long as the solution works according to the chain of architectural principles, and it satisfies the needs as addressed in the requirements, it will solve the problem and we can call it an architecturally valid solution.

To emphasize the difference between requirements and principles, principles concern *how* things are performed, while requirements concern *what* needs to be performed to solve the problem. Principles provide a basis for dispersed but integrated decision making, and can serve as the tie-breaker in settling disputes. They address the perpetual management problem of influence at a distance. Principles motivate requirements. Requirements motivate the structure and content of the solution.

Requirements are very different from principles as they serve a very different purpose, but they do go hand in hand within well-architected solutions. Table 10 compares some aspects of principles and requirements.

Architectural Requirements

Table 10: Principles versus requirements

	Principle	Requirement
Purpose	Essential approach to achieve a certain goal. The embedded rules how things are meant to work in the future. Drives choices.	Specification of what the solution must satisfy to meet the goal. The source that tests if the solution satisfies the requirement (i.e., solves the business problem). Ensures choices made are present in the solution.
Property	Aims for durability by nature (problem changes do not necessarily change all principles).	Shorter-lived by nature (problem changes are reflected in the requirement, based on principles).
Syntax	The present tense of the future state (facts, sequential actions, planned events, etc.). Cannot be omitted (words like *can, might, maybe, etc.* are not used). States a future fact	The imperative mood of something that solves a problem. Uses words like must, should, etc. Stated as a directive (something that must be realized to meet the future state or fact).

How Requirements Relate to Principles

Principles put measure and realism into requirements. As with principles, architectural requirements are truly essential. As said before, 'architectural' means that there is only one acceptable way to it. Doing things differently solves a different problem. By now, we can see that principles give a better understanding and scoping of the problem and feed the requirements; that is, the principles create context and relevance for the requirements. A well-founded solution that fully addresses the problem at hand is based on both requirements and principles. The relation between a principle and a requirement is depicted in the diagram in Figure 32.

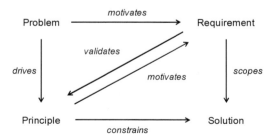

Figure 32: Relationships of requirements

A Simple Example

In practice, multiple principles can motivate one or more requirements; a single principle, however, can also motivate multiple requirements (for example, when multiple sub-solutions are involved). Figure 33 illustrates this characteristic.

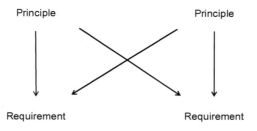

Figure 33: Principle(s) motivate requirement(s)

A fully elaborated architecture blueprint contains requirements; in the architecture blueprint methodology in ITSA requirements are documented as a separate deliverable. Later we will see that this document is motivated by goals, principles, and standards that are documented in the Solution Overview of the architecture blueprint and provides a context to evaluate the relevance of the elicited requirements.

A Simple Example

To give an easy-to-understand example of how problem, principle, requirement, and solution work together, it is best to use a simple everyday life example:[45]

Goal (the problem)	'I need to move myself.'
Principle	'We move by man-power.'
Requirement	'It must operate in room temperature environments.'

For this combination of goal, principle and requirement we can think of some typical solutions:

Solutions	'Roller skates, bicycle, walking, swimming, etc.'

---

[45] The formulation of full-blown principles goes beyond the objective of this chapter. This is only intended to demonstrate the difference between principles and requirements.

If a second requirement were to state 'It must move me up the hill,' it would rule out the 'swimming' solution, because water somehow always seems to flow down!

This example demonstrates that principles are concerned with how things need to work. They express the embedded rules, mechanics, techniques, and so on. Requirements, on the other hand, are concerned with what needs to be performed to solve the problem, i.e. they represent the behavior of the solution. A simple IT-related example looks like this:

Business goal	'Increase profitability by 10%.'
Business principle	'We use a web-channel as an additional sales channel.'
Business requirement	'The web-channel must have a lower cost of sale than current channels.'

In the same context, suppose a technical principle constrains the solution to use one technology platform. A sample principle and requirement for the implementation view could then be:

Implementation principle	'We use Microsoft .Net as our application platform.'
Implementation requirement	'MS Commerce Server must be used for web transactions.'

How Others Treat Requirements

In a proper architecture process, requirements should be derived from principles in the architecture. The same principle may give rise to different requirements when it is part of different architectures. Requirements are refined in the process of gaining stakeholder ownership by revisiting both principles and requirement over and over again. This process typically ferrets out the essentials of the problem and is in great contrast to the classical requirements-gathering methodologies that cannot – as explained previously – guarantee relevance and completeness.

The activity of requirement elicitation, representation, and validation, therefore, is intertwined with the creation of architectural principles. This is very different from many architecture methodologies that take requirements as a starting point. We could question whether these methodologies are truly architectural or merely design activities disguised as architecture. It is not uncommon that stakeholders throw in as many requirements as possible,

Conclusion

independent from each other, trying to scope the solution. This is rooted in the misconception that more detail is better. But more detail can lead to multiple and contradicting interpretations, which do not guarantee success. If good requirements engineering is all we need, why do we still have so many projects that are destined to fail from the start? This could well be the root cause of such problems. Requirements elicited through requirements engineering fundamentally lack the structure and coherent weight that they would have when they are derived from architectural principles, especially from ITSA principles.

Conclusion

Requirements are distinctively different from principles, but they are as essential as principles. Requirements have a very different purpose than principles have. Both have their own very special role in the architecture process and the development lifecycle. Architectural requirements differ from project requirements in the sense that they scope the solution, while the latter focuses on the interior of the project. We looked at the interrelationship of requirements and principles within the context of the problem and the solution. From the way we weave requirements elicitation and principle creation together, we have a different view on architecture methodologies: is it truly architectural, or is it design in disguise?

13. Putting Everything Together

> *The shortest distance between two points is a straight line,*
> *except in a bent universe.*
>
> ~Theo de Klerk

Architecture is about making essential choices in defining a solution to a business need. A common language makes it possible to create a bridge between the business need and the IT solution. Gradually, taking well defined steps, we work towards the right 'DNA' for a realization project. We start with a first draft, the architecture concept, and depending on the level of detail needed, we evolve it into a fully elaborated architecture blueprint. This involves validating and justifying principles, models, standards, and requirements of the solution together with estimating its costs and assessing its feasibility. With this fully scoped and constrained solution, the realization project can look for fitting and necessary details, and allow the sponsor to possibly send out a Request for Proposal for realization of the IT solution.

IT Architecture starts when we begin to craft an IT solution for a business problem and this solution must take into account the many different facets posed by the various stakeholders. Architecture work ends, or at least goes into maintenance mode, only after the solution is implemented and operational. To make architecture real, we need an approach and associated framework to consolidate the architectural findings and choices. For this, we talked about the ITSA framework and its architectural elements. These all link together into a seamless chain of justification for a solution that solves the (business) problem at hand.

Now the real challenge is how to apply the architecture to realize the operational solution. After all, architecture is a means to an end and not a goal by itself — we don't do architecture for architecture's sake but to solve business problems. How do we ensure that everyone is on the same page during its implementation (design, build, test, deployment)? Moreover, it is not uncommon that third parties will get involved for implementation projects, which can require painstaking procedures to send out Requests for Proposals. Implementation parties need to be constrained by the architecture, but they also need freedom to propose a solution based on their own expertise, best practices, and applied technology, to optimally address the business problem and its associated drivers and goals. The architecture must have a sufficient level of completeness and detail to safely start the realization work such that the products being delivered are in line with the proposed solution concept and solve the problem in the intended way.

During the realization project and after the final deployment of the solution, the architecture may be challenged on its correctness. The realization project might encounter unforeseen problems requiring architectural wisdom from the architect to satisfy implementation aspects without degrading the solution. Likewise, changes in the environment might evolve the architecture to include enhancements. The process that controls, maintains, and enforces the architecture is called *IT architecture governance*.[46] Part of this process is also the encouragement to re-use and leverage earlier concepts and frameworks, and to learn from mistakes.

This chapter discusses how we refine and enhance the first drafts of the architectural elements from the ITSA framework into a fully elaborated architecture blueprint together with the aspects of IT architecture governance.

Bridging the Gap

Architecture is the means to ensure that the business needs and IT are aligned and rooted in the business goals. It is also about ferreting out the essentials, while leaving all other matters to the subject matter experts farther down the realization stream. Therefore, there is a line where architecture stops and design begins. The line is not always sharp, but the results of architecture are the basic building stones, as illustrated in Figure 34, on which, and boundaries within which, the design is made and implementation is built. Rather than aiming for the ultimate, grand, complete architecture from Day One, the architecture framework allows for a two- or multiple-pronged approach: get the most essential elements first, and then go for the others. This incremental approach is not unknown in software development, and it works equally well for architecture. The first incremental cycle delivers an initial architecture that covers the main topics, and that broadly outlines the future direction and desired end state. This allows for enough information and evidence to make decisions on whether to move forward or reconsider the desirability of the end state – for reasons of cost, feasibility, possibility, and others.

---

[46] This is not to be confused with IT governance (which includes IT architecture governance), which has a different purpose.

Bridging the Gap

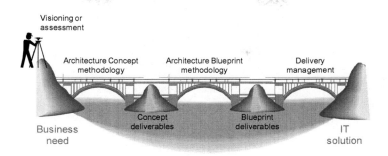

Figure 34: Bridging business and IT through architecture

This first cycle in the ITSA approach is called the architecture concept, and it is limited in time, effort, and scope, and likewise has limited results. But it is an ideal vehicle to quickly assess the problem domain and define major choices for the future solution that solidly addresses and supports the business drivers and goals. Within a few weeks, a first draft is available on which to build further or to reconsider. It doesn't take months or a year of investments before we know if the architecture and its solution are addressing the right issues. But the rough sketch is insufficient to start a design phase.

In the initial architecture concept cycle, the business goals and drivers are defined and the ITSA framework is filled with principles, models, and standards. This gives us a sense of how the final solution will look. The rough data from the architecture concept must be further sculpted, enhanced, verified, and made (more) complete. The subsequent incremental cycle or cycles are meant to do just that. These cycles are a more thorough undertaking and the time needed is determined by the scope and effort to complete the architecture. Or at least complete it to the point that (part of) the solution can be handed over to the design and implementation project activities. In each of these cycles, the following steps need to occur:

1. Scope and delimit the problem and its solution.
2. Gather and confirm information from all stakeholders, and investigate existing (re)usable material from any existing architectures (e.g. enterprise architecture), the problem domain and the trends in this domain.
3. Define a solution concept based on the gathered information and material.
4. Specify the problem to be solved as exactly as possible.

5. Use the problem specification to specify the solution as exactly as possible.
6. Create a high-level plan based on the dependencies between solution parts and experience needed.
7. Document the findings and specifications.

These steps are initially sequential, but insights during later steps may influence and redefine some of the findings in earlier steps. This iterative and also partially heuristic approach is fully natural to architecture, and within ITSA it is known as *architecture blueprinting*. In practice, this follows the business approval; architecture blueprint deliverables feed the design process and the development of, for example, the Project Initiation Document (PID) in the PRINCE II project management methodology.

The architecture blueprint process and its deliverables that fully describe the solution in an architectural way:

- Ensure that both the client and the delivery team are confident about proceeding.
- Tie all technical and implementation choices back to a business need.
- Demonstrate that the content and structure of the solution are necessary and sufficient.
- Provide the basis for detailed design and implementation work.
- Make possible an accurate assessment of the project scope and feasibility.
- Assure a shared understanding of and commitment to the solution by all stakeholders.
- Integrate ITSA with classic project management methodologies such as PRINCE II or company-specific ones.

The ITSA architecture blueprint deliverables are the link that connects the architecture with the follow-on realization work (design, build, deploy, etc.). They contain:

- Essential information for designers and builders to make tradeoffs in their approach and technology.
- Information about the solution (purpose, function, interfaces, components and relationships, principles of operation, properties, means of constructing and testing).

- Information represented as principles, models, standards, requirements and additional texts.

It is very important to realize that the ITSA architecture blueprint is architectural in nature and therefore not a detailed cookbook. Remember the 'everything you need nothing you don't' mantra that is so persuasive in architecture work. Therefore, an architecture blueprint does not contain:

- Decisions that are not essential for the IT solution.
- Information that is commonly known by system builders and component suppliers.

Traversing the Gap

In the previous section we saw that the ITSA architecture blueprint phase bridges the gap between the assessment of the initial business need and the final aligned IT solution deliverables. These deliverables are realized through traditional project management. As we briefly introduced in Chapter 4, the architecture blueprint further elaborates the results of the architecture concept into the architecture blueprint deliverables Solution Overview, Architectural Requirements, Features and Functions, Architectural Design, Acceptance Criteria, Feasibility Assessment, and a preliminary Project Plan. Together, these architecture deliverables provide the basis for development and deployment of the solution. Figure 35 illustrates how the ITSA views motivate deliverables of the architecture blueprint, which in turn feed design project deliverables. For the sake of clarity, we assume a full blown architecture engagement with follow-on project. Depending on the scope, size, and environment of the project, some parts of the architecture blueprint may be executed to a lesser extent as we will see.

The architecture blueprint deliverables can be divided into two sets: one that elaborates on the contents of the solution and one that is more about the process for managing and verifying the realization of the solution. A good architecture blueprint cannot do without addressing the process aspects involved; remember that the road towards project success may be strewn with political and cultural issues. This combination of architectural descriptions and the accompanying architecture process has proven to be very effective.

Putting Everything Together

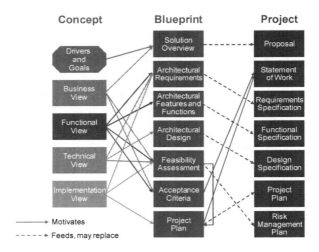

Figure 35: The big picture from initial architecture to solution project

Architecture Blueprint Deliverables

In this section, we will describe each of the architecture blueprint deliverables. Depending on the decided time, effort, and scope, each of these deliverables may be developed in full for an extensive solution, or some may be combined for a smaller-sized solution. This decision is also influenced by the choice of the development approach, such as waterfall, incremental, iterative, time boxed, or other. It is not uncommon for the content of the architecture blueprint deliverables to be influenced by factors such as the involvement of other methodologies. The architecture blueprint methodology is flexible and can accommodate such factors. It is like a painter's palette for the architect. The main thing that must not be lost is the intent and purpose of the architecture blueprint deliverables, the type of information that is essential to capture and use. The wrapping or presentation of this information in other deliverable formats is less relevant.

Deliverable: Solution Overview

Purpose	Describes the problem and proposed solution. Creates a fully defined solution concept that contains: • A complete elaboration of the architecture concept output. • Full depth and breadth of the four ITSA views.

Architecture Blueprint Deliverables

Audience	Business sponsor, CIO/CTO, line of business VP, co-architect, co-project manager, designers. Third parties in Request for Proposal initiatives.
Description	Expands the output of the architecture concept. Is not merely a transfer of information from the architecture concept capture to the Solution Overview. It includes the elaboration of the principles and models with all their implications, obstacles and actions. Fills in details overlooked or not addressed in the architecture concept.
Organization	Organized according to the four ITSA views. Specifies principles (their rationales, implications, obstacles, and actions), models, and standards. Provides a foundation for all subsequent architecture blueprint deliverables: • Principles will drive later requirements. • Technical and implementation models will be the basis for the solution design.
Design handover	This deliverable is the basis for the solution design. All essential decisions that the solution must obey are documented in the principles, models, and standards. This deliverable is the 'constitution' of the solution.

Deliverable: Architectural Requirements

Purpose	Describes the business requirements imposed on the solution: what the user *must* be able to do with the solution.
Audience	CIO/CTO, line of business VP, co-architect, co-project manager, designers, solution providers. Third parties in Request for Proposal initiatives.
Description	Where the architecture principles, models, and standards in the Solution Overview allow a certain freedom to the designers, requirements impose a further restriction on the behavior of the solution based on specific requirements. Architectural requirements are about the perceived business usage, value, and outcome of the solution. As such, these requirements are of a higher level than functional or technical requirements in which the business is not and should not be interested. The requirements are always rooted in principles, models, and standards. During talks with stakeholders, requirements may also be specified, but they must have a firm grounding in principles. Requirements that are already specified before the architecture must be shown to fit within the architectural framework. If not, these requirements should be discarded. In some cases they may highlight a missing part in the architecture. In that case, additional principles and/or models must be added to the Solution Overview. These new additions must fit within the framework through their rationales. This document, together with the Solution Overview, Solution Features & Functions, and Solution Design documents form the basis for third parties to submit proposals in response to a Request for Proposal process.

Putting Everything Together

Organization	Organized according to four views of ITSA Provides a foundation for all subsequent architecture blueprint deliverables: • Requirements will drive later Acceptance Criteria. • Requirements will drive later Features & Functions.
Comments	These requirements are called *architectural* to set them apart from other requirements, such as *project* requirements, that deal with issues (such as development environments, staff skills, etc.) that in and by themselves have no residue in the final solution and its behavior.
Design handover	This document specifies the *must have* features, both functionally as well as technically, of the solution. These features must be demonstrable in the final solution. The high levels as well as low level design documents are ruled by the requirements. Any proposal document from third parties for the design and implementation must address each of the requirements specified.

Deliverable: Architectural Features & Functions

Purpose	Elaborates the features and functions of the solution in sufficient detail for stakeholders to have a complete and accurate description of how users will interact with the solution. Provides information for assessing the acceptability of the implementation of the solution.
Audience	Co-architect, co-project manager, designers, solution providers Third parties in Request for Proposal initiatives
Description	Specifies what the solution looks like *externally*. Specifies how users interact with the solution to satisfy requirements. Lists the mandatory features and functions (often a subset of the requirements). Does not specify deliverables. Can be presented as a set of use cases.
Organization	Scenario's will drive later Architectural Design.
Design handover	The user interaction described in this document leads to further elaborated use case descriptions with additional scenarios. These in turn will lead to class identification, collaboration, and interaction diagrams. In the early stages it also leads to prototyping of (graphical) user interfaces.

Deliverable: Architectural Design

Purpose	The Architectural Design communicates: • How the solution is structured. • How the solution operates to provide the required functional capabilities.
Audience	Co-architect, co-project manager, designers, solution providers. Third parties in Request for Proposal initiatives.

Architecture Blueprint Deliverables

Description	Expresses a high-level description of the solution.
	Focuses on the technical and implementation views of ITSA.
	Does not describe detailed design issues, such as the user interface in terms of what buttons and sliders to incorporate in the user interface – that is designer's work.
	Can include technical and implementation models addressing pervasive attributes, business scenarios, and business processes.
Organization	Design components and dependencies will drive the Statement of Work section of the Project Plan.
Design handover	The Architectural Design information motivates the technical design documents. It identifies packages, modules, distributed computing requirements, interfaces, security, normalization of data, distribution, and implementation of the graphical interface.

Deliverable: Feasibility Assessment

Purpose	Captures open issues from the prior architecture blueprint deliverables in one place.
	Assesses whether it is possible to deliver the proposed solution, focusing on the identified open issues and actions, unconfirmed assumptions, known dependencies and risks, and other potential failure modes.
	Helps the sponsor to understand the issues.
Audience	Architect, project manager, business sponsor, CIO/CTO, line of business VP (to decide how to handle and finance the issues), co-architect
Description	This deliverable serves two purposes: one for the sponsor and one for the party that potentially implements the solution.
	The solution must present a viable business proposition in order to continue. Issues in this respect include:
	• Organizational readiness – does the organization have the budget, project support resources, complete and correct understanding of its business problems and the desired solution?
	• Architectural readiness – is the architecture well defined, complete enough, implementable, and properly aligned with the client's business need?
	• Implementer readiness – does the implementer have the skills and resources to deliver? Does the project advance the implementers strategy?
	Addresses the issues:
	• Open issues and actions
	• Unconfirmed assumptions
	• Known dependencies and risks
	• Other potential failure modes
Organization	Feasibility issues will drive the risk management section of the Project Plan.

Putting Everything Together

Design handover	The elements of this deliverable motivate the risk assessment and mitigation parts of the Project Plan. Actions are defined to overcome each of the perceived problems or incapability's. Insurmountable problems will need to be addressed first and require CIO level attention, as they may be showstoppers and may need to lead to part-solutions, different solutions, and organizational changes to remove the problems, or a no-go decision.

Deliverable: Project Plan

Purpose	Communicates: • Project goals and the means to achieve them • Resources required (time, money, personnel) • Milestones achieved or to be achieved • Assumptions made • Project risks and associated risk response plans
Audience	Delivery project manager (who will fill in the dates and resources) Solution provider management (who approves the plan) Sponsor (who buys into the plan) Project teams and program managers
Description	Is a major document used by project teams in designing, implementing, and supporting client solutions. Outlines activities, resources, and issues relevant to the project.
Organization	Scope and Work breakdown structure Activities and estimates Schedule Resources Project communication, documentation and reporting Project risks Project processes (change management, escalation, acceptance etc.)
Design Handover	This deliverable is largely created by the (proposed) project manager with input from the IT architect based on the content of the other architecture blueprint deliverables. Typically the Feasibility Assessment is used to do this, but the obstacles and implications elaborated on in the Solution Overview are also pivotal to complete the project plan deliverable; they lead to a first definition of the work breakdown structure.

Governance of IT Architecture and IT

Once the architecture is complete, the temptation exists to cast it in stone and 'throw it over the wall' to the people farther down the stream of realization processes (like design, build, and implementation). This is a similar attitude to what was done in the past when (thick) specifications were written and subsequently handed over to the next group. That attitude caused lots of problems as the implementers interpreted the specifications in their own way and made changes along the way because the technological world around them was changing. Without knowing the fundamental choices rooted in the solution architecture, their well-intended changes might lead the solution in a different direction than the business problem it was supposed to solve.

If there is one thing we learned from that past, it is that individuals (e.g. architects) who are at the root of the problem and solution description should stay in touch with the solution during its entire lifecycle – from inception to deployment.

- They must ensure that the solution stays on the architectural track and delivers what it is supposed to deliver.

- They must be able to answer any question others may have on the 'what and how' of the solution – issues that shaped the architecture of the solution.

- Most importantly, they must have the flexibility to revise the original concept if reality shows that this originally good idea proves impossible to realize. In those cases, a new approach must be conceived that remains true to the business drivers, goals and the solution principles derived from them. The modified solution architecture stays on target.

Therefore, an IT architect's job is never done. His involvement will decrease over time during the design, build, and implementation phases, but he keeps in touch with what's going on and also ensures that developments are in line with the architecture that was set up. In the final delivery phases, the involvement of the architect increases again when he must ensure that the architectural requirements are all present and accounted for in the final solution.

The process known as IT architecture governance maintains, enhances, modifies, communicates, reuses, and enforces the architecture. This ensures that the business goals and stakeholder interests are served properly and have a clear accountability and (delegation of) authority in this process. This IT architecture governance can only work well if it is treated like a living organism, continuously fed with monitored information from the solution projects under way, stakeholder feedback on usability and value creation.[47]

---

[47] The TOGAF documentation treats this in more detail in Chapter 26 of the (online) TOGAF 2006 (V8.1.1) edition *(http://www.opengroup.org/togaf)*.

Putting Everything Together

This is made possible if the entire IT environment is under governance. The IT architecture governance is then part of IT governance, as illustrated in Figure 36.

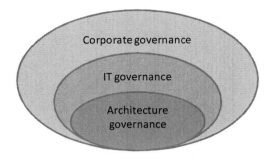

Figure 36: IT governance and architecture governance

Some significant writings on IT governance have been done by Weill and Ross.[48] They specify the act of IT governance as 'specifying the decision rights and accountability framework to encourage desirable behavior in using IT.' Their research showed that firms with an explicit, recognized, known, and executed IT governance, linked to corporate governance,[49] were more successful than those without such a process. Such an IT governance framework helps to address the three fundamental questions for business-IT alignment:

- Are we doing the right things (based on organization goals, coherent and consistent initiatives): vision and strategy?

- Do we do them in the right manner (efficient, productive, prioritized, interlinked projects that do not work against each other): focus areas and spearheads?

- Do we execute them the right way (consistent, correct implementation following set rules and methods): projects?

For each of these questions, we need to define processes and determine:

- Who is accountable for them (plus lines of delegation)?

- Who provides input to them?

- Who makes the day-to-day decisions within them?

---

[48] Weill, P., Ross, J.W., (2004). *IT Governance*. Harvard Business School Publishing, Boston.

[49] Corporate governance looks after the key assets of the company – one of them being the IT and information assets, next to human, financial, IP, physical, process and relationship assets.

The IT governance process guards and feeds the IT architecture on all levels: enterprise architecture on a corporate level, solution and infrastructure architectures on lower levels. The architectures are kept in line with the corporate strategies and objectives and change when they change. The industry has formal open standards based IT governance processes and frameworks in which IT architecture governance can be embedded:

- COSO – Committee of Sponsoring Organizations issued 'Internal Control – Integrated Framework,' aimed at measuring effectiveness of operations, reliability of financial reporting, and compliance with laws and regulations.
- ITIL – IT Infrastructure Library. Best practices for IT service management (ITIL V2) and covering the entire services lifecycle (ITIL V3).
- CobiT – Control Objectives for Information and related Technology. A comprehensive framework defined by ISACA (Information Systems Audit and Control Association) for assessing, establishing, and evaluating IT governance throughout the entire range of IT related activities from strategy to operational tasks.
- BiSL/ASL – Business Service Library/Application Services Library – a Dutch initiative to separate processes, concerns, and stakeholders with a business-functional management interest from those that are more concerned with application management.

Prepare for the Future and Use the Past

One aspect of IT architecture governance is the fact that one should learn from the past and not attempt to reinvent wheels. Wheels are plentiful – either within the local organization or outside. Architectures set up for certain solutions addressing specific business needs can be reused in part or in full for new or complementary solutions within the same problem domain. The whole process does not need to start from scratch.

Figure 37 shows the general process of architecture development. On the left, we see how enterprise architecture inspires and limits the options of a solution architecture, which in turn results in a solution based on and compliant with the solution architecture. By removing all project (engagement) specific elements from these three architectures, we can obtain a more generic reusable architecture or solution that is *project independent* or even *project agnostic*. Adding the specific needs and requirements of another project to these reusable elements results in new instances of the solution architecture or solution.

Putting Everything Together

The great thing about starting with reuse is that one can basically start on any element of Figure 37. If a lower element exists, with some reverse engineering one can define a more generic, higher up element. If we make it project specific, we move from right to left. If we make it reusable, we move from left to right by removing project-specific items. For example, if a solution is already present, its architecture can be reverse engineered: what fundamental principles, models, decisions were used to make the solution the way it is. This makes up the solution architecture. When we remove the project specific parts, it becomes a reference solution architecture. This reference architecture can apply equally well for situations in, for example, the banking industry for both banks A and B. But once the specifics of bank B have been added, we have a solution architecture that is only useful for bank B.

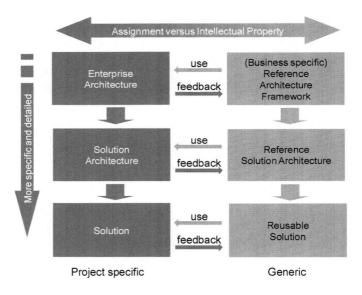

Figure 37: Reuse and actual use

It will be clear that IT suppliers and partners will focus more on reusable elements to assist their different customers. After all, anything that can be reused already has a lot of experience and a best practice embedded from previous engagements and provides a head start for a new engagement. Creating these reference architectures does not come for free. A formalized knowledge capture and reuse process must be in place and endorsed, in which architects are given time (and budget) to enrich the collection of reference architectures. Once in place, a reference architecture allows us to:

Conclusion

- Harvest the knowledge and experience of the solution team that created and implemented the defined solution architecture.
- Facilitate (and sometimes endorse) the use and application of reference solution architectures.
- Embed a knowledge capture and reuse process into architecture engagement processes.
- Evolve and develop the contents according to new insights.
- Enable community building in domains of interest.

The architecture blueprint collateral that is developed in an engagement is an ideal starting point for creating reference architectures. The principles, models, and standards defined in the architecture concept and subsequent architecture blueprint can be sorted back into the four ITSA views and made project-independent. This process is illustrated in Figure 38. Architecture blueprinting processes must actively leverage existing reference architectures by reusing them and adding client specific elements.

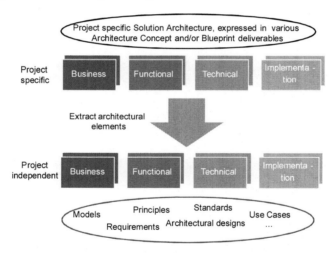

Figure 38: Extracting architectural elements for reuse

Conclusion

All the details of the ITSA framework and the architectural elements (like principles, models, standards, and requirements) have come together in this chapter, where we put them in the context of the architecture methodologies that build on the ITSA framework. We bridge the gap between business need

Putting Everything Together

and IT solution through a gradual process that works from the first draft (the architecture concept) into a fully elaborated architecture blueprint. The architecture blueprint deliverables allow for better detailed constraints of the IT solution, but also to create the right ingredients for the follow-on realization project. In fact, they enable a gradual handover that gives the project manager good insight into what is needed to start up a healthy project. Architecture work does not end when the project has started, because good governance is needed to keep the architecture accurate and up-to-date. Moreover, architecture work does not end when the project ends. Generic concepts can be derived from the architecture deliverables to create a reference architecture that can be adapted for similar IT solutions.

14. Architecture and Project Management

> *The single best payoff in terms of project success comes from having good project definition early.*
>
> ~RAND Corporation

Projects only have a chance to succeed if the proper starting conditions are met. The project scope is the result of an effective architecture process, directed by the architect and the client. The project managers use this scope, and other project parameters such as budget, time, and quality, to determine the project constraints. An integral approach, in which the project manager is a key stakeholder in this process, is the only feasible way to deliver a project that meets both architecture and realistic project constraints. Project management and architecture have a common interest to create a successful solution. However, architecture and project management have very different purposes. The architect works with the business sponsor on the content of the IT solution – what must the solution do? The project manager is entrusted by the sponsor with the resources to realize the solution – how to get it done?

Projects are human creations and, in some respect, they also have human traits. These traits manifest in initial conditions defined at the start of a project and those that will arise during the life of the project. If the initial conditions are wrong, the project has no chance of success. Architecture obviously is the right instrument to create the right initial conditions – the right 'DNA' – to ensure that the project fits the business need and provides necessary information to the project manager. Events during the project life can influence the project in both positive and negative ways. These must be handled by proper project management and governance to keep the project delivering on its promises. Good project management is a necessity for this.

In the preceding chapters, we discussed the characteristics of the concept of architecture and what actually makes up the architecture. Except for the notion that stakeholders play a necessary role in the process of defining the architecture, until now we did not explore how project management relates to the architecture process. It must be clear that the concept of architecture is a necessary prerequisite to project management activities. More specifically, managing realization project activities to design, build, and deploy artifacts; in short, realization activities. The central question, then, is how principles, models, standards, and requirements find their way through to the solution we had in mind. As we explained earlier, the role of the architect is mostly to make the right inferences from the business/stakeholder needs and find possibilities that result in an architecture that adequately addresses those needs. If we distinguish between architecture work and realization work, legitimate questions arise about the relationship between architecture and project management. Do the two overlap? Are they complementary? Is one part of the other? Can one do without the other? Let us examine how architecture and project management work together in an engagement.

The Role of Project Management

If we want to clearly understand what project management entails, we need to understand what defines a project. One of the major characteristics of a project is that it has a distinct beginning and end – a finite endeavor, so to speak. The result of a project is one or more products (such as a piece of software, a service, or a technical infrastructure). What makes a project special is that it is a one-time temporary endeavor with very different management dynamics compared to the sustainable, stable management processes in organizations. Project results are usually handed over to these organizational processes. Although the objective of a project can sometimes even be reorganization, the project results are always part of a bigger management system to which it is accountable.

To manage a project properly, achieving the project goals and objectives from the sponsor's point of view, the project manager has to work within a defined scope, stay within budget, and deliver on time the products against the quality agreed upon.[50] Where does the project manager find the information needed to manage the scope, budget, time, and quality that determine the project constraints? Let us look more closely at this question:

- **Scope** – The project scope very much depends on what problem the project needs to solve. Maybe the project is part of a bigger whole, such as a program. In both cases, can the project manager know how the project can positively contribute, in part or in full, to the solution of the sponsor's business problem?

- **Budget** – Getting a clear picture of the resources (people, materials, etc.) needed to successfully run the project depends heavily on what will be used to create the solution; i.e. what makes up the solution.

---

[50] Of course the project manager faces many other challenges, such as politics, resource optimizations, cultural aspects, etc. However, for our purpose of elaborating on the architecture versus project management relation, we limit our discussion to these constraints.

Even the financing model itself can be part of the solution in some cases. Can one properly plan project resources without knowing the technicalities and implementation constraints of the solution?

- **Time** – The order in which different parts of the solution are to be implemented is often a careful balance among technical necessities, resource availability, and possibilities of the operational environment to absorb the solution. How can the project be managed in a way that provides the best organizational absorption and most efficient resource deployment?

- **Quality** – A direct result of the requirements gathering and analysis process is the quality imposed on the solution. These results are input to various implementation activities (design, testing, etc.), including the management aspects of the project. How can the design and test activities properly be done without knowing the architectural requirements of the solution?

We can safely say that managing a project, in general, is about keeping the project within the scope, ensuring that the project structure covers every architectural element defined, securing funding and staffing, delivering the project results on time and against the agreed upon acceptance criteria. As the list above unmistakably reveals, architecture is the only source from which these project constraints can be derived.

Architecture from a Project Management View

The previous paragraph demonstrates that the process to define project constraints involves dealing with many ambiguities and uncertainties. To provide the right ingredients to manage a project successfully right from the start, we need a heuristic approach in order to know the purpose, boundaries, requirements, etc. of the solution. We would be running in the dark if we start a project without knowing these constraints. The concept of architecture and its process provides us the heuristics to find out the real business/stakeholder needs and to define a solution that effectively solves the problem within the organizational context.

In Chapter 1, where we introduced the concept of architecture, we elaborated on architecture essentials and the fundamental differences between architecture and design. The architecture process is about getting a grip on the real problem and finding the constraints wherein a solution can be created in order to guide design and deployment activities that follow. A natural follow-on process is to organize a temporary endeavor, which we call a project.

Architecture and Project Management

The initiation of a project has totally different dynamics than the precursor architecture process. While the architecture process aims at making sense and meaning to the stakeholders in the context of problem and solution definition, the project management process focuses much more on creating a controlled environment that gets the work done. Project initiation, therefore, focuses on getting the right conditions (people, resources, timing, etc.) wherein the project can be a success. Let us revisit our earlier list of questions on project constraints with a complementary architecture view:

- **Scope** – Through the four ITSA views, we investigate the complex needs of all stakeholders. We simply cannot address a functional need without involving any implications from a technical or implementation perspective. The same applies to obstacles. If the project is part of a bigger whole, the architecture process will unravel it, and will make the project manager aware of the real scope of the project. The coherency of the ITSA framework simply prevents anything from being left out of the project scope. This is a big advantage for the project manager when initiating a project based on architectural coherency. The architecture is the best instrument to manage scope through the entire lifecycle of the solution.

- **Budget** – The principles, models, and standards from the architecture process lead us to a well-defined view on the technicalities and implementation constraints of the solution, while the architectural requirements clearly prescribe any performance and capacity characteristics that the solution needs to fulfill. This should give the project manager enough insight to work with subject matter experts to properly size the project and come to a fair estimation of the budget needed.

- **Time** – The result of the ITSA framework's implementation view is the insight from various stakeholders into the order in which solution components can be built and implemented. From a project management perspective, the architecture process provides the insight on how the solution can be deployed. The architecture process is a highly interactive process, with many stakeholders involved, and it facilitates a joint learning exercise for both the people using and benefiting from the solution as well as the people who have to make the solution happen. Put differently, we have much more insight into the way and extent the organization is able to exploit the solution. Project managers have more at hand to fairly estimate the time and sequence to build and deploy the solution if they are part of a preceding architecture process.

- **Quality** – The architectural requirements that are elicited during the architecture process are the foundation for a project's Requirements Specification.[51] We can give in to the temptation to specify all sorts of requirements in the project, but if these requirements do not contribute to the purpose of the solution, they are a waste of time and effort. Architectural requirements, therefore, help us to initiate a project that will also solve the problem for the project sponsors. It can be very frustrating to finish a project and discover that it does not solve the problem the project was intended to solve. And don't forget the political hurdles the project will face when trying to implement something that doesn't help to cure the pain! With the architectural requirements at hand, we can create a requirement specifications document that helps us to test quality issues that must be addressed to solve the problem. In an early stage of the project, we already have insight whether the project results will be a success to the sponsor.

We see from this list that the concept of architecture is a major contributor to the creation of a successful project. Actually, one cannot do without the other. Without project management realism about whether things are indeed deployable and/or manageable, project failure is inevitable. Likewise, if a project is initiated without a firm grounding in scope, budget, time, and quality aspects, we are witnessing the start of yet another project that is heading towards disaster.

An Integral Approach

It must be clear that the concept of architecture and project management have a distinct and also necessary relationship. It escapes logic why project management methodologies do not take architecture deliverables into account. The architecture process is all about what is needed to solve a problem, while the process of project management safeguards the delivery, establishing the solution concept according to constraints like, scope, budget time and quality. In short, architecture directs us what to do; project management enables us to get it done. A comparison is given in Table 11.

---

[51] See for more details Chapter 12 on Architectural Requirements.

Architecture and Project Management

Table 11: Architecture versus project management

Architecture	Project Management
Defines the scope of the engagement	Keeps engagement within scope
Articulates the essential elements of the solution, work to be done	Ensures that the work breakdown structure covers all essential elements
Defines resources needed to complete the work	Ensures that staffing, funding, and resources are available to support work
Defines acceptance criteria for solution iterations and phases	Defines milestones and schedule, ensures that the acceptance criteria are met

We see that there is a clear difference between architecture and project management; likewise, there is a clear difference between the roles of the architect and the project manager. By nature, the architect's relationship with the project sponsor concerns the content of the solution. The architect serves the sponsor in the sense that he defines a solution that exactly fits its purpose and does not overdo the solution. The architect should serve as the rock of integrity here, guiding the follow-on processes such that they result in the solution as it is defined in the architecture. In that respect, the architect serves all stakeholders, and the sponsor in particular. After all, the sponsor brought the problem to our attention.

The project manager has a very different relationship with the sponsor. The sponsor basically bets his money on the project manager and trusts that he can do the job for the money budgeted. While the architect is fully accountable for the end result solving the sponsor problem, the project manager is fully responsible for getting the job done with the means and resources provided. In essence, the architect is the agent of the sponsor, while the project manager is the agent of the builder. Knowing this, it is no surprise that so many IT projects fall short in practice, as this role difference is not recognized.

We deliberately favor an integrated approach, in which architect and project manager work closely together, while maintaining their distinct roles and responsibilities. There is no way an architect or project manager can do both project management and architecture at the same time without being caught in a conflict of interests. Project management and architecture are two very different disciplines with opposing dynamics, each with its own special skills requirements. Of course, there are occasions where the two roles can be combined in one person, but these are very simplified endeavors.

During the architecture process, the architect leads and guides the team of subject matter experts to define the solution. The project manager is a subject matter expert and key stakeholder in the implementation view.

Conclusion

Architect and project manager work together to define an architecture that has sufficient of realism that it really can be implemented instead of becoming a paper exercise that collects dust on a bookshelf. During the architecture process, the project manager can assess the feasibility of the solution and help the architect avoid mistakes in terms of implementation aspects.

During the realization activities, the architect can help the project manager to avoid mistakes in early stages of the project that would lead to unwanted results. Figure 39 depicts the various relationships among the architect, the project manager, and the business sponsor.

From the previous discussion, we can see that the business sponsor has a different interest in the architecture and project management processes. They are complementary to each other and both are needed by the business sponsor for a solution that fits his needs. Unlike many architecture philosophies, our approach focuses not only on the architecture content aspects, but also on the architecture *process* aspects. By no means is architecture just about creating a technical artifact. The project manager is a natural stakeholder representing the builder during this architecture process.

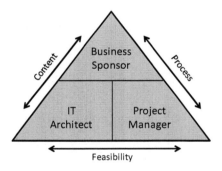

Figure 39: Relation architect, project manager, and business sponsor

Conclusion

The project parameters scope, budget, time, and quality play a key role in defining a successful project. Project management methodologies lack the mechanisms to provide information to set these parameters in an accurate manner. It is the architecture process that enables the project manager (as a key stakeholder) to obtain the proper information needed to define the project. Architecture and project management serve very different purposes, but they are very dependent on each other. The architect maintains a relationship with the business sponsor that focuses on the content of the

Architecture and Project Management

solution, while the project manager's relationship with the sponsor concerns the project process for managing the resources that make the scoped project stay within budget, be delivered on time, and deliver the agreed quality.

15. The IT Architect Profession

> *Your profession is not what brings home your paycheck. Your profession is what you were put on earth to do. With such passion and such intensity that it becomes spiritual in calling.*
>
> ~Vincent van Gogh

Developing IT architecture skills is not easy because they draw upon many disciplines. Building up the necessary experience takes a while; one does not become an IT architect overnight. Besides holistic knowledge and insight, many of the competences concern accountability. The architect must not leave behind an unrealistic or unjustifiable solution that would break down at the first unforeseen event. The maturing architect profession is now developing certification programs that look for evidence of architectural experience; nowadays this experience is a necessity, as the impact of the architect is growing as enterprises are becoming more complex.

There are many opinions on what exactly constitutes IT architecture, and the profession of IT architecture. It must be clear by now that practicing IT architecture is not just the management of some project management lifecycle model that calls for the creation of architectural artifacts. Unfortunately, the latter is still the dominant view in the architecture discipline. The focus of the architect really must be on the heuristics for creating those architectural artifacts. Architects should address the real concerns the sponsor faces and create space to address these concerns, instead of simply concentrating on the content of architecture frameworks. They must claim their true role in the business-IT relationship, a role that is both existential and meaningful to the business. Only through this behavior can architects truly contribute to the value IT can bring to the business.

In discussions about the IT architecture profession, it is not uncommon to reflect on the concepts and profession of physical architecture. There is a very simple reason for this: in essence they both pursue similar goals and need similar skills to achieve these goals.

The practice of physical architecture involves a large number and variety of often complex skills and disciplines, ranging from the technical considerations of structural engineering, environmental services, and energy conservation to the functional considerations of room layout, interior design, and human comfort. Similarly, the evolution of the IT industry resulted in information and technology related constructions that are becoming increasingly more complex. This naturally raised the demand in the IT industry for individuals who can deal with this complexity and understand the art of creating structures to address this complexity. It makes sense to have a closer look at the skills of a physical architect and how they fit the necessary skills for the IT architect.

Vitruvius

Marcus Vitruvius (1st century BC) was a Roman writer, architect, and engineer and is the author of *De Architectura*, known today as *The Ten Books on Architecture*. This is the only surviving major collection on architecture from classical antiquity and contains a great fund of information on architecture and its practice. In fact, Vitruvius was the first theorist on the concept of architecture and is famous for asserting that a structure must exhibit the three qualities of *firmitas, utilitas, venustas* – that is, it must be strong or durable, useful, and beautiful. These three qualities can also be applied to the IT related architectures and can be seen as the basis for practicing the art of architecture. Although it was long ago that Vitruvius defined competences for the architect,[52] they still can be seen as paramount for the architecture profession. We don't need much imagination to translate these into the competences of what we recognize today as an IT architect, as shown in Table 12.

Of course, the competences specified by Vitruvius must be seen from a historical perspective, and today's IT architect has more and sometimes other skills in his/her toolkit. Knowledge and experience of the business domain, knowledge and experience of the IT domain, experience in consulting and communication, and skills in using modern methodologies and techniques are just a few aspects that would characterize the competent IT architect today – as illustrated in the third column of Table 12.

Clearly, what we can learn from the above is that the IT architecture profession is an interdisciplinary field that draws upon science, technology, sociology, politics, art, etc. and is often governed by the architect's own personal experience, approach, and philosophy. Accountability is an important part of many of these competences; the architect must not deliver

---

[52] See extracts of books I and II of *De Architectura*, http://www.humanistictexts.org/vitruvius.htm

Vitruvius

an unrealistic or unjustifiable solution that would break down at the first unforeseen event. The architect is accountable at all times and must stay in touch with the project while the solution is being built. The IT architect profession is challenging as it encompasses different disciplines and varying roles the architect has to play.

Table 12: Perspectives on architect competences

Competence	Vitruvius' perspective	IT architect's perspective
Creative and apt in the acquisition of knowledge	(Undetermined)	IT architects must be creative and commit to lifelong learning to keep up with new developments, apply new insights and experiences
Good writer	Commits observation and experience to writing, in order to assist memory	IT architects need to be good communicators and document the agreed architecture and the reasons and experience behind it
Skillful draftsman	Representing the forms of designs	IT architects must be able to visualize the architecture solution in models and sketches
Versed in geometry	The use of the right line and circle, the level and the square, whereby the delineations of buildings on plane surfaces are greatly facilitated	IT architects must apply the right components to create the solutions, taking into account their characteristics such as functionality, compatibility, usefulness and others.
Optics	Judgment of the requisite quantity of light, according to the aspect of a building	IT architects make optimal use of the environment to fit in the solution
Expert at figures	Arithmetic provides cost estimates, and aids in the measurement of works; assisted by the laws of geometry	IT architects make estimates of the type and amount of resources needed to design and build the solution
Acquainted with history	Justify the use of many ornaments that may be introduced	IT Architects leverage on previous experiences, existing frameworks and de jure and de facto standards
Informed on the principles of natural and moral philosophy	Teach the architect to be above meanness, avoid arrogance, and be just, compliant and faithful to a client	IT architect apply fit-for-purpose and work in the clients interest
Somewhat of a musician	Assists an architect in the use of harmonic and mathematical proportion	IT architects focus on essentials, incorporating the right amounts of required components to define a fitting solution
Not ignorant of the law and of physics, nor of the motions, laws, and relations to each other, of the heavenly bodies	Astronomy instructs an architect in the points of the heavens, the laws of the celestial bodies, the equinoxes, solstices, and courses of the stars	IT architects are aware and take into account the various forces and stakes of stakeholders in defining a realistic and operational solution.

The IT Architect Profession

What Characterizes the Profession of IT Architect?

Every IT architecture engagement starts with a problem. At some time, somebody somewhere will express a need for a solution that involves IT. This is where the challenge for the architect starts. We have to frame the problem without restricting ourselves to our own familiar frames of mind. The architect sometimes has to go to areas where no one has gone before. Many questions must be answered. How is the problem stated? Are there already requirements? Are they really addressing the problem? Is this the individual that owns the problem, i.e. the sponsor or major stakeholder?

Without an architectural perspective that inherently views a problem from multiple concerns,[53] we will very likely hear only one perspective of the problem. A problem in the view of the individual might very well be just a symptom whose root-cause lies in another problem. The architect must be skilled in correctly framing the problem. Time and effort are needed to get acquainted with the whole context to take a holistic approach to clearly define the problem, such that it is recognized by all stakeholders, and most importantly by the sponsor.

The architect must oversee many different domains, manage the separation of concerns through the stakeholders, and be able to create abstract representations of what is going to be designed and built. The IT architect must be capable of handling multiple dimensional aggregations:

- What is the highest level in motivating the architecture?
- What architecture motivates 'downstream' work?
- What constitutes the follow-on architectures?

For example, a technical perspective of an enterprise architecture could very well be a directive (business view) for a technology architecture. From an this perspective, there can be a cascade of architectural layers as is shown in Figure 40. More precisely, the needs (functional view) of one architecture become the reasoning of another one.

The previous discourse demonstrates only half of what the architect encounters in his work: creating artifacts that form the groundwork for choices that are fundamental for follow-on work. The other half of the architect's work involves coping with politics, culture, and sense making.

---

[53] See Chapter 1 on one of the key aspects of architecture: the separation of concerns.

Am I Doing Design or Architecture?

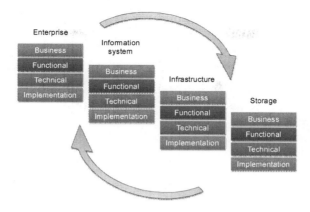

Figure 40: Cascading architectures

The key message here is that practicing architecture is not a labeling exercise to fill in an architecture framework, but a sensemaking process that serves all stakeholders to define an IT solution that is designable, buildable, and implementable. It can be just a 'simple' cost reduction that drives this process, or more complicated matters such as enterprise innovation. This sensemaking process is paramount; important in this approach is that the definition of the problem is done together with all stakeholders. Many political and cultural issues sometimes need to be addressed to find the real answer to the essence of the problem and its prescription in the IT solution. This is the heart of the profession, whether the solution impacts the entire enterprise through solution architecture, constitutes an overarching solution for a business problem through enterprise architecture, or requires a technology solution through technical architecture.

We see that the architect must have extensive skills and experience to fulfill his role. In addition to these so-called 'soft' skills, the architect must also keep up with horizontal (technology) development and vertical (business) expertise. For example, an architect who is working with networks in the telecommunication (Telco) market must acquire and maintain both network and Telco-market knowledge and apply Telco related architecture frameworks such as eTOM.

Am I Doing Design or Architecture?

Discussions on the architecture profession frequently raise questions regarding the difference between design skills and architecture skills. Are they the same? Do they overlap? The answer is that architects create the guidance (architecture work), while consultants and engineers fill in the details (design work). In smaller institutions, people might perform a mixture of the two, but that has the inherent danger of favoring one over the other. Each role has a distinct function in creating a solution for a client, and each demands different behavior, competences, and skills.

There are fundamental differences between what architects and designers do, although they sometimes can be perceived as subtle. The designer seeks to find the optimal solution to a well understood problem. This endeavor is more science than art, algorithmic in nature, and deals mostly with a system's measurable attributes. The architect, on the other hand, deals primarily with non-measurable attributes using non-quantitative tools and guidelines based on practical lessons learned; that is, the architect takes a heuristic approach. Whereas designers and engineers are primarily working deductively, architects are primarily working inductively.[54] This doesn't mean, however, that the architect never uses quantitative tools and methods, or that the designer never uses a heuristic approach.

In architecture, the essentials of what is being described are dictated by the stakeholder needs and are expressed as principles. A different architecture therefore implies that different needs are being addressed; that is, it solves a different problem. It is the architect's job to set the boundaries or scope for a project. The designer can consider many different solutions to address the same need, and within the same scope. For example, there are many designs/products that the designer can apply to address the need for an e-mail solution within an enterprise.[55]

It is the architect's role to make the right inferences from the business/stakeholder needs that result in an architecture that adequately solves them. The designer focuses mostly on making the correct decisions from a rich palette of choices allowed by the architecture (for example, what technology will work in the environment being designed). In short, an architect focuses on fit-for-purpose, while the designer focuses on optimization.

Another key skill of the architect is the 'art' of developing architectural principles. It takes a profound effort to craft and fine-tune principles that describe the fundamental approach to address the needs the solution must satisfy. The architect must include a lot of context and meaning to create durable principles that contain the embedded rules of how things will work in the future. Typical aspects the architect considers in this process are: will it work tomorrow? Is it limited to only one technology? What are the effects on

---

[54] Rechtin, E., Maier, M. W. (1997), *The Art of System Architecting*, CRC Press LLC. London.

[55] Rivera, R(2007), Am I Doing Architecture or Design Work?, *IT Professional, vol. 9, no. 6, pp. 46-48, Nov/Dec, 2007,* IEEE Computer Society.

other systems or the business environment? Would this at all be achievable at this moment in time, or within the current organizational setting? This shows the architect's focus on essentials, coherency, and solution-fit.

Most design methods start from requirements,[56] and the designer must have the skills to elicit requirements that describe what the solution must satisfy to meet its goal. The designer needs 'material' expertise – the subject matter expert – to later develop the specifications and models in the various domains. For example, starting from an IT consolidation's requirements, the designer needs to define the method's phases, develop specifications and models for servers, storage, network, security, and so on. Basically, a designer can use the same architecture to create another solution with newer technology if it (the technology) becomes out of date and still solves the same business problem that is addressed by the *old* architecture. We see that, over time, the architecture doesn't change as frequently as designs do; therefore we can say that the architect is more long-term oriented than the designer. Table 13 summarizes the comparison of architect and designer.

Table 13: The architect versus the designer

The Architect	The Designer
Ferrets out the essentials dictated by need	Makes choices that are compatible with the architecture
Addresses a need with only one single architecture (different need implies a different architecture)	Can create many different designs that address the same need
Endeavors to make the correct inferences	Must make the correct decisions such that his choices address the need
Seeks to find a fit-for-purpose	Optimizes the way technology is applied

The Architect Career Path

IT architects need a broad set of skills together with a lot of knowledge – most of all experience about what is do-able with current and near-future technologies, etc. Acquiring that knowledge and experience takes time and effort. Mastering the IT architect profession therefore is not a clear-cut career evolution. As Marcus Vitruvius stated, 'successful implementation is founded on the imperative that the materials chosen can be worked to completely fulfill their purpose. This is impossible without mastery of both

---

[56] There is a distinct difference between requirements and architectural requirements; see chapter 12.

theory and practice. Consequently, a person who is not familiar with both cannot make any claims to the title of architect.'

Being an IT architect means we have the knowledge and have experience in applying that knowledge. As an IT architect, we are expected to give guidance in a broad range of technologies and practice a broad range of skills. This means we must have experience in the range of technologies we are using to architect the IT solution. How else can we make good judgment on the architectural elements that imply choices for follow-on design work, and so on? The obvious question, then, is how does one become an architect?

Our discussion so far implies that the best way to become an architect is to gradually climb the experience ladder. But the great variety of aspects needed to master the profession of architect asks for a lifetime of experience. We suggest starting by specializing in areas of designing or engineering. Apart from the content, skills are developed that are applicable to other areas as well. When moving over to another area it takes much less time to adopt new knowledge and skills. Gradually people start learning leadership skills that are broadly applicable like for instance to lead a project or part of it.

We assumed that the precursor activities an architect does are of technical nature; hence architects have a technical background. As today's awareness rises about what architecture can do for us and the way the profession starts maturing, we begin to see that there are different types of architects. As an example, within HP the architecture program differentiates among architects that focus on Technology, Solution, or Enterprise:

- Technology Architects – Practitioners who define architectures that apply to a particular knowledge domain (information, application, infrastructure) and its deployment into an operational environment.

- Solution Architects – Practitioners who define architectures of an information system and/or service and its effective deployment into an operational environment to solve a key business problem.

- Enterprise Architects – Practitioners who define architectures of an enterprise's information systems and their effective deployment, operation, and evolution to enable the business.

It might become customary that architects who have more affinity towards business than technology will not necessarily have a long standing technical background. Their knowledge and experience might come more from the business domain or information management domain or from the area where social meets technical. What creates the common ground among all different types of architects is the ability to take a holistic view of the problem at hand and use a heuristic approach to ferret out the essentials to solve the problem.[57] As in most architecture, there is no one vantage point from which the whole structure can be understood;[58] therefore, the architect must use these abilities within the context of views and stakeholders.

Certification

If we consider the essential skills and accountability of the architect we presented here, we come to the notion that choosing the right architect for the job is a serious matter. As high impact professions mature, accreditation or even certification becomes customary. Within the field of IT architecture there have been many developments on the subject of certification. We must distinguish here between certifications that focus on the knowledge of architecture-related methodologies, frameworks, tools, etc. (such as TOGAF certification),[59] and certifications that assess the proven abilities and skillfulness of an IT architect applying IT architecture successfully.

The architect profession within HP has adopted two certification programs for practitioners:

- The IT Architecture Certification (ITAC) program from the Open Group[60]
- The Microsoft Certified Architect program[61]

Both programs have similar requirements for skills and experiences. The Open Group's program is agnostic in terms of technology, frameworks, methods, and products, whereas the Microsoft program has requirements that relate to Microsoft technology. Common in both programs is that candidates must demonstrate evidence of experience in architecting IT solutions and possess strong technical and leadership skills. They should master effective communication with business, architecture, and technology professionals. Microsoft states that it expects 10 years of experience, whereas

---

[57] Holistic in the sense that the scope of concern can still be limited, but the architect takes into account surrounding influences and matters.

[58] Marcus Vitruvius (1st century BC), *The Architecture of Marcus Vitruvius Pollio in Ten Books translated from the Latin by Joseph Gwilt*, London, John Weale, 1860. See also http://www.humanistictexts.org/vitruvius.htm

[59] TOGAF is The Open Group Architecture Framework for enterprise architecture and has dedicated certification. See http://www.opengroup.org/togaf/cert/

[60] The Open Group IT Architect Certification program http://www.opengroup.org/itac/cert/

[61] The Microsoft Certified Architect Program http://www.microsoft.com/learning/mcp/architect/default.mspx

The IT Architect Profession

the Open Group requires 3 years of experience *producing* IT architectures. The candidates are required to pass a rigorous review board interview conducted by experts in the discipline of IT architecture.

Certification within HP is part of the career path of the architect, and it is a necessity and prerequisite to grow towards senior levels in the architect job function. The certification process and criteria of the Open Group ITAC program are added to the Technical Career Path (TCP) framework HP uses to maintain job level development for the non-managerial job domains. The Open Group has recognized and accredited the HP architect certification program, which therefore has ACP (Accredited Certification Program) status.

The Open Group ITAC Program

The ITAC program recognizes three distinct levels of certification:[62]

- Certified IT Architect – The candidate is able to perform with assistance/supervision, with a wide range of appropriate skills, as a contributing architect.
- Master Certified IT Architect – The candidate is able to perform independently and take responsibility for delivery of systems and solutions as lead architect.
- Distinguished Certified IT Architect – The candidate has significant breadth and depth of impact on the business through the application of IT architecture.

To recognize the deviations that individuals typically experience in their career path, the certification for ITAC level 3 (Distinguished Certified IT Architect) defines three Career Path Categories: Chief/Lead IT Architect, Enterprise IT Architect, and IT Architect Profession Leader.

IT Architects who are certified within the ITAC program are allowed to use the Open Group ITAC logo on their business cards, etc.[63]

The Microsoft Certified Architect Program

The Microsoft Certified Architect program consists of two sets of certifications. One set is for architects who specialize in Microsoft

---

[62] Information Technology Architect Certification Certification Policy November 2007 Version 1.4 *http://www.opengroup.org/itac/cert/docs/ITAC_Certification_Policy.pdf*

[63] Information Technology Architect Certification (ITAC) Conformance Requirements *http://www.opengroup.org/itac/cert/docs/ITAC_Conformance_Requirements.pdf*

technology, where the architect can currently certify in three disciplines (messaging, databases, and online transaction processing – OLTP).

The other certification program Microsoft offers is for architects who possess broad architecture skills and apply a variety of non-Microsoft and Microsoft technologies to deliver client solutions. This program recognizes certification in the field of IT infrastructure in areas such as network, security, storage, network operating systems, and certification for architects who create IT solutions like integration, workflow, and applications.

Conclusion

The skills of IT architects draw upon many disciplines. The IT architect profession is challenging, as it also involves various roles and a great amount of accountability towards the stakeholders of an IT solution. The writings of Vitruvius teach us that the skills used in the world of physical architecture shed light on what typically characterizes the profession of an IT architect. The architect must bridge many different domains and manage the separation of concerns through the stakeholders. Knowing the content is one thing; many of the architect's skills also concern handling politics, good communication, and various soft skills. Still, the architect must act as the rock of integrity towards all stakeholders and the sponsor. It is a natural development in this maturing profession that certification programs on demonstrating skills develop, going beyond simply being knowledgeable about the subject. More and more the notion arises that the work of an IT architect is of a very different nature than the work of a designer. The necessity for multi-disciplinary skills and behavior to bridge various communities makes the IT architect profession very special indeed.

16. Resources for IT Architecture

We are just statistics, born to consume resources.
~Epistles

There are many resources for the multi-disciplinary IT architect. In addition to the tons of information accessible through search engines, high-quality information is available from the various communities and institutes that specialize in IT architecture.

In the past, collecting information about certain topics was largely a question of who we knew and what libraries and books we could use. The Internet has made finding information about anything much easier, although not all information is equally trustworthy or reliable. Searching on 'IT architecture' will result in a great many hits, not all useful. Consider the lists below as our personal best finds, starting points from which, no doubt, new pointers will lead further.

Links

The problem with providing Internet links is that some of these links change frequently. A fundamental principle as 'A URL once issued will always remain the same' seems against human nature where reorganizations and renamed units result in a new web structure that reflects this. We all know that putting significant information in unique keys is a bad thing to do as significance may change. But it is easier to remember. So for what it is currently worth, here are some pointers. Searching for the institution names may help to find the new location in case the link is broken.

- www.amazon.com – the location to look for any book published in the English language and currently available. Search for 'IT architecture' or 'enterprise architecture' and a long list of books will come up, complete with lists of similar books, and reviews of users who liked or disliked the book for various reasons.

- www.archimate.org – website for information on the enterprise architecture modeling language ArchiMate. Including stencils for

Resources for IT Architecture

Visio if we don't use a formal modeling tool such as Aris, BiZZdesign, or SystemArchitect. The modeling language has been adopted by The Open Group.

Books

Books on IT architecture are plentiful. A search on www.amazon.com will confirm this. Not all are equally useful, but some are gems. The books below are not in any particular order of preference, but have been found useful by the authors. More details can be found in their entries on Amazon.

- The Art of Systems Architecting, by Mark W. Maier and Eberhardt Rechtin, published by CRC Press LLC. ISBN: 0849304407
- Manage IT as a business – survival, by Mark D. Lutchen, published by John Wiley & Sons, 2004, ISBN 0-471-47104-6. About IT enabling and empowering the business.
- Enterprise Architecture At Work, by Marc Lankhorst a.o., published by Springer, 2005, ISBN 3-540-24371-2. Describes the application of the 'ArchiMate' modeling language for architecture, currently controlled through The Open Group. User's website at www.archimate.org
- Dynamic Enterprise Architecture: How to Make It Work, by Roel Wagter, Martin van den Berg, Joost Luijpers, and Marlies van Steenbergen, published by John Wiley & Sons, 2005, ISBN 0-471-68272-1. Description of an architectural methodology defined by Sogeti
- The Speed of Trust. by Stephen Covey, published by Simon & Schuster, 2006, ISBN 0-7432-9560-9. Description of ethical behavior, integrity, trust issues architects will have to address.
- Building Agreement, by Roger Fisher and Daniel Shapiro, published by Random House, 2007, ISBN-13 978-1-905-21108-1. About negotiation skills and getting to compromises
- Enterprise Architecture Planning, by Steven H. Spewak, published by John Wiley & Sons, 1992, ISBN 0-471-59985-9. Older book based on Zachman 's top two layers (ballpark/owners view) defining an enterprise architecture.
- IT Governance, by Peter Weil, Jeanne W. Ross, published Harvard Business School Press, 2000, ISBN 1-59139-253-5. About IT

- Constructing Blueprints for Enterprise IT Architectures, by Bernard Boar, published by John Wiley & Sons, 1999, ISBN 0-471-29620-1 Based on Zachman framework, describes EA blueprinting process and templates. Good first two chapters, goes overboard in the rest where enterprise architecture gets inundated by documentation and paper tigers.

- TOGAF™ – 2009 Edition (incorporating V9), by The Open Group, published by The Open Group. Downloadable PDF from www.theopengroup.org/catalog or on paper ISBN 9789087532307. Formal manual on the TOGAF enterprise architecture methodology of The Open Group.

Journals

- Microsoft Architecture Journal – The journal contains many generic architectural topics unrelated to specific Microsoft technologies. http://msdn2.microsoft.com/en-us/arcjournal/default.aspx

- ArchiMate Newsletter – free PDF downloadable from www.archimate.org

- The Journal of Information Architecture – A peer-reviewed scholarly journal that started in spring 2009. Its aim is to facilitate the systematic development of the scientific body of knowledge in the field of information architecture. http://journalofia.org/issue/

- Journal of Enterprise Architecture – Paid online member of the Association of Enterprise Architecture is required to download the PDF articles. http://www.aeajournal.org/

Communities and Institutes

- The Open Group (www.opengroup.org) – The Open Group has a number of forums and areas that are dedicated to IT Architecture. Noteworthy are:
    - The Architecture Forum of the Open Group that has developed and evolves a framework for enterprise

Resources for IT Architecture

   architecture (TOGAF). A certification program supports the framework. (www.opengroup.org/architecture)
   - The ArchiMate Forum which is the platform for the use and evolution of ArchiMate, an open and independent modeling-language for enterprise architecture. (www.opengroup.org/archimate)
   - The IT Architect Certification program that is dedicated to the certification program of the IT Architect. (www.opengroup.org/itac)
- The Institute for Enterprise Architecture developments (IFEAD) (http://www.enterprise-architecture.info/index.htm). IFEAD is an independent research and information exchange organization working on the future state of Enterprise Architecture.
- Federated Enterprise Architecture Certification, FEAC (www.feacinstitute.org) – The FEAC™ Institute, in partnership with the California State University at East Bay and the National University in San Diego, prides itself on being the premier Certification Institution for Enterprise Architects.
- The TM Forum's Business Process Framework (eTOM) (http://www.tmforum.org/BusinessProcessFramework/1647/home.html) is known around the world for the common vocabulary it establishes for both business and functional processes.
- The social network site LinkedIn has a number of architecture related groups:
  - The IT Architect Network, http://www.linkedin.com/groups?gid=100988
  - The Enterprise Architecture Network, http://www.linkedin.com/groups?gid=36781
  - Model Driven Architecture Network, http://www.linkedin.com/groups?gid=50539
  - Information Architect Network, http://www.linkedin.com/groups?gid=80164
  - TOGAF for Architecture, http://www.linkedin.com/groups?gid=67926
  - The Service Oriented Architecture Special Interest Group

Appendix A – SWOT Analysis for Drivers and Goals

The SWOT analysis (which stands for Strengths, Weaknesses, Opportunities, Threats) is a tool that originated in the strategic management discipline. It is used to plan strategies for an enterprise, but it has also demonstrated its value in architecture engagements. If there is a lack of clear statements to define the business drivers and/or goals, it helps to find the direction an enterprise foresees in the short or long term. Having these elements is important for creating the right architecture. After all, the entire ITSA approach is based on stakeholder participation to achieve the set business goals.

A SWOT analysis is often shown as four quadrants – one for each of the four elements, as we see in Figure 41.

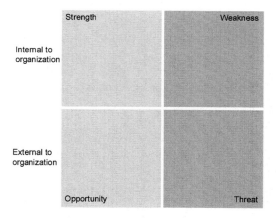

Figure 41: SWOT analysis chart

The entries in Strength and Opportunity indicate the strong points of the organization on which they can capitalize, whereas the entries in Weakness and Threat indicate the weaker points against which the organization must protect itself (but at the same time may indicate areas for improvement). The SWOT analysis is an answer to the 'Where are we now?' question. By combining entries in different quadrants, we can make statements that answer 'Where do we want to be?'

The SWOT Focus Areas – Where Are We?

The four focus areas of SWOT are briefly explained below, indicating the types of statements expected in each of the four quadrants.

Appendix A – SWOT Analysis for Drivers and Goals

Strength

Strength entries indicate the internal capabilities and resources of the organization: why the organization has been successful in certain ways, relevant to the problem area for which we seek to define a solution architecture. Some questions that will lead to Strength entries are:

- What are the organization's core competencies?
- What specific, unique, or special knowledge or skills are engrained in the organization?
- What successful processes and tools does it employ?
- What is the external image and reputation of the organization that shows its success?

Weakness

Weakness entries indicate the not-so-successful working of the organization, the internal liabilities. In a way, the Weakness area contains entries that express the opposite of the Strength entries. As such, they represent potential drivers that are inspirational of what needs to change: goals to work on. Some questions that will lead to Weakness entries are:

- What are our main liabilities?
- What specific knowledge or skills are missing or underdeveloped?
- What processes don't function well or are missing?
- What is the external image and reputation of the organization that shows it weakness?

Opportunities

Opportunity entries provide ways to capitalize on the strength of the organization in opening up new ways of doing things – new, improved, more efficient, and more profitable. Some questions that will lead to Opportunity entries are:

- Have opportunities already been identified? Which ones?
- What existing products or processes can be improved?
- What skills and knowledge do we have to realize new opportunities? Can we capitalize on what we already have in place?

Appendix A – SWOT Analysis for Drivers and Goals

- What opportunities will open up if a weakness can be eliminated or reduced?

Threats

Threats are external events which are not fully under the organization's control, such as customer behavior, competitor behavior, environmental regulations, market imposed regulations, and such. Similar to the ITSA principle's obstacles, threats will lead to goals that reduce or remove such threats. Some questions that will lead to Threat entries are:

- What (current and expected future) obstacles are hindering current progress?
- What external regulations might impact the current business?
- Where will the organization be negatively impacted if changes were introduced?

The SWOT to Identify Business Drivers and Goals

When the four quadrants of the SWOT analysis have been populated, they provide a view of what successful strategies for the (near) future will be in the problem area for which we seek a solution. We can combine elements of two quadrants to use them in the best way possible. Table 14 summarizes all possible combinations of two quadrants.

The SWOT derived goals can be refined by transferring them into one of the four perspectives of the Balanced Score Card (financial, customer, process, and innovation) as explained in Appendix B. The advantage of the transfer is not only in the balancing of the goals within and between the four BSC perspectives, but also to add specific targets and measurements to them which makes these goals SMART.[64] If there are too many goals, they can be ranked according to stakeholder perception such that we focus on the most important and relevant goals. From Table 14 we see that the Strength-Opportunity cell entries are the easy ones to realize, while the Weakness-Threat ones will be most difficult or will require some pre-conditions to be realized first. Often in SWOT analysis, the focus is on the black-bordered top right quadrant combinations to derive goals and drivers.

The SWOT analysis gives a good start to elicit the raw material that can be used to define the ITSA business drivers and business goals. This process,

---

[64] Specific, Measurable, Achievable, Realistic, Timebound – see Chapter 5 on business drivers and goals.

Appendix A – SWOT Analysis for Drivers and Goals

as depicted in Figure 42, gives more insight into what the organization's real problems are and where opportunities for good IT solutions exist. When used together with the Balanced Score Card, it leads to strong ITSA business drivers and goals.

Table 14: SWOT quadrant combinations

	Strength	Weakness	Opportunity	Threat
Strength How to make the most out of these?	-	Employ strength to reduce or **remove** weakness Usually medium-long range efforts	Employ the strength to **pursue** new opportunities These are readily available and can address short and long term opportunities	Employ strength to reduce or **eliminate** some threats
Weakness How to reduce these and turn them into strengths?	-	-	Long term **improvement** when able to reduce weaknesses that will then enable opportunities	Develop strategies **to mitigate** the risks imposed by threats partly because of identified weaknesses The latter could be remedied or reduced in significance to battle threats Dependent on Strength-*other* cell implementations first
Opportunity How to realize this within our power?	-	-	-	Capitalize on opportunity that **reduces** the significance of threats Medium-long range efforts – dependent on Strength-*other* cell implementations first
Threat How to eliminate these or be able to minimize impact?	-	-	-	-

Appendix A – SWOT Analysis for Drivers and Goals

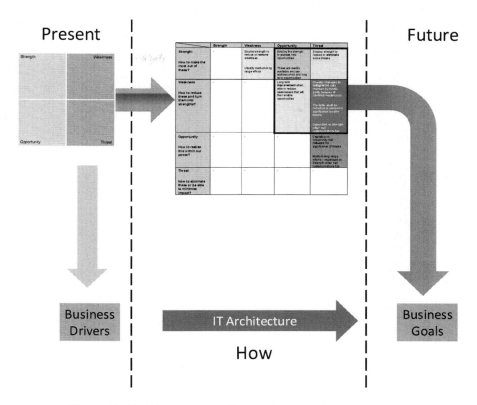

Figure 42: SWOT as a start to elicit raw business drivers and goals

Appendix B – The Balanced Score Card for Topic Areas

The Balanced Score Card (BSC) represents interrelated performance elements for an enterprise. If changes in the enterprise require IT architecture, the BSC provides a useful means for deriving ITSA topic areas.

The Balanced Score Card

Robert Kaplan and David Norton first introduced the Balanced Score Card in 1992 in the Harvard Business Review journal as a means of performance measurements. Later articles on the application and experiences of the BSC evolved into a book, exploring the new synthesis of the historical-cost financial accounting model with long range competitive capabilities for information age companies.[65] Since then the BSC has been widely applied, and best practices around the BSC can be found in many books and documents.

> 'The balanced scorecard retains traditional financial measures. But financial measures tell the story of past events, an adequate story for industrial age companies for which investments in long-term capabilities and client relationships were not critical for success. These financial measures are inadequate, however, for guiding and evaluating the journey that information age companies must make to create future value through investment in clients, suppliers, employees, processes, technology, and innovation.'
>
> ~Kaplan and Norton

The Balanced Score Card is an organization-oriented tool: it maps the strategy and vision of an organization into (smaller scaled) vision-aligned operational goals and actions for various perspectives – financial as well as for human resources, processes, and growth.

In addition to translating organizational vision into operational goals, the BSC is foremost a means of information and communication of what the organization stood for, stands for and will stand for: its vision and strategy. It

---

[65] Kaplan, R.S. & Norton, D.P. (1996). *The balanced scorecard: translating strategy into action.* Harvard Business School Press, Boston, MA 02163.

Appendix B – The Balanced Score Card for Topic Areas

does this by analyzing the organization from four different perspectives and results in instructions for each of these to realize that vision and strategy.

A stable organization balances the activities in each of the four perspectives.[66] Over-achieving or over-emphasizing elements in one of the perspectives makes the organization unstable. This is the third aspect of BSC: it provides feedback loops to ensure that the achievement of operational goals in various perspectives influences the other perspectives. This results in adjustments of those perspectives and possibly the strategy.

A BSC is also a useful means to derive ITSA topic areas because any change of the organization to re-find, regain or remain (in) its balance means that one needs to focus on certain elements that will drive changes in the organization. The topic areas are then closely associated with these elements.

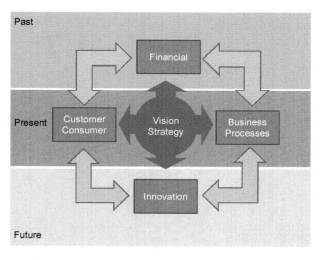

Figure 43: Balanced Score Card

The BSC uses four perspectives in which organizations can state their vision and strategy and translate them into actions to make it happen. These four perspectives are:

- **Financial** – Short range. What do stakeholders expect of us? How can we express all activities in a common measurement unit such as money? What does each activity contribute? What are current financial indicators? Is there a need for additional ones such as cost/benefit rather than plain profit or ROI?

---

[66] The BSC terminology uses the word 'view' here also. To avoid confusion with the four ITSA views, we prefer to call the BSC views 'perspectives.'

Appendix B – The Balanced Score Card for Topic Areas

- **Customer/Consumer** – Medium Range. What does the customer or consumer expect us to deliver, and in what quality? An organization cannot force the customer, but it has all the means to find out what he needs and wants and how to 'lure' him to do business with the organization. Without appropriate attention, consumers will move their business elsewhere and sales figures will decline. Poor performance in the consumer perspective is an indication of decline, even if this is not reflected yet in financial figures.

- **Business Processes** – Medium Range. What processes does the organization use and how well do they work in relation to what customers expect or require? Do they help to run an efficient business with the right mix of people, resources, and methods? Actions and measurements in this perspective require that they are defined by internal people with intimate knowledge of these processes.

- **Innovation** – Long Range. How does the organization learn from current trends? And how does it anticipate changes in the future with regard to demand, technological progress, or changing regulations by adapting its processes, services, and educating its staff accordingly? How does the organization grow, learn (this includes mentoring people), facilitate communication between groups, and remain effective? This aspect is important in many of the knowledge-worker type organizations.

For each of these four perspectives, a number of goals (typically five to seven) are defined to realize the strategy and vision. These goals are agreed upon by stakeholder (manager) consensus, and where there is any interdependency between goals (in the same or other perspectives), this is indicated. These goals are described using objectives, measures, targets, and initiatives:

- Objectives: what do we want to achieve?

- Measures: what KPIs (key performance indicators) do we use to determine where we are?

- Targets: what is the ultimate KPI value we want to reach?

- Initiatives: what activities do we deploy to enable our objectives?

Any improvement of performance in one of the perspectives most likely has an impact on elements of the other three perspectives. For example, where the Innovation perspective recognizes new insights on conducting business,

Appendix B – The Balanced Score Card for Topic Areas

this affects the processes. Then processes will, in turn, affect the way customers can be served (and who will respond to this), and this will affect our financial position. Some examples of KPIs are listed in the next call-out.

The way the organization's vision and strategy translate into actions in the four BSC perspectives is heavily dependent on the people running the organization. An organization itself has no mission or vision. The people who make up the organization determine this vision and therefore determine the way to translate this into actions based on their organizational culture and position in society. Of course, no BSC software will do this. It can only assist the organization in documenting and monitoring its vision.

> **Examples of KPIs**
>
> Examples of KPIs found in case studies and literature (browsing the web) include:
>
> **Financial**: Cash flow, return on investment, return on capital employed, return on equity, economic value added, days sales in receivables, days in payables, shareholder loyalty, market value add, profit as percentage of sales, gross margin, dividends
>
> **Customer**: return-business (loyalty), new clients, client retention, client demographics or segments, purchase behavior (per demographic group), bad debts, profitability by client segment, alignment client requests and offerings, client complaints, market share, client visits, client size
>
> **Business Processes**: Number of activities, opportunity success rate, accident ratios, equipment effectiveness, automated entry and approval, manual vs. IT run processes, community involvement, patents pending, labor utilization rates, waste reduction, space utilization, breakeven time, client request response times
>
> **Innovation**: Investment rate, illness rate, accidents, training effectiveness, training hours, internal promotions %, employee turnover, work environment quality, gender/diversity ratios, employee satisfaction, knowledge management, ethics violations, internal communication, leadership development, motivation, employee suggestions

The BSC and topic areas

Given an existing BSC for an organization, its goals stated in its four perspectives and the initiatives defined are ideal hunting grounds for finding the right topic areas that matter – as they will be in line with the business-defined strategy and goals. The BSC goals that are set in any of its four

Appendix B – The Balanced Score Card for Topic Areas

perspectives (to address the organization's vision and strategy) result in objectives and initiatives. For a future business situation with IT as supporting or enabling component, most of the relevant BSC goals that are useful for IT architecture will be rooted in the customer, process, and innovation perspectives because these are related to current and future positions. They are less rooted in the financial perspective as this perspective is always working on historic data. These initiatives and their impact on and change of the current situation are sources of topic areas. This process is depicted in Figure 44. Table 15 gives some examples of topic areas based on a selection of the sample KPIs listed earlier.

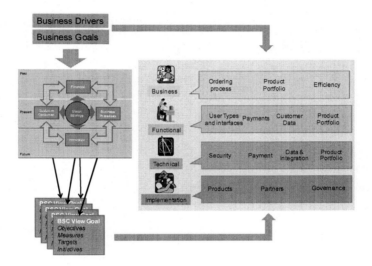

Figure 44: Balanced Score Card provides topic areas

Note that not all KPIs have an IT component and therefore may not result in a topic area, whereas some KPIs may result in the same topic area. Also depending on organizational maturity, different topic areas may apply to specific organizations.

BSC and Product Selection

The BSC can also be useful when IT product selections are required. Often this comes as part of the implementation view, or it is requested without a full-blown architecture engagement. In these cases, the 'why' questions of the business view as well as the 'what' questions of the functional view are important to ensure that the right product is selected from a business-

Appendix B – The Balanced Score Card for Topic Areas

functional point of view, whereas the 'how' and 'with what' questions of the technical view and implementation view are relevant to ensure the fitting business tool also fits the IT environment in which it must operate. For all four ITSA views, basic principles on what makes a product fitting can be derived from specifying the right topic areas and thinking about the main concerns within them. Again, the KPIs of existing BSCs may assist us to focus on the right topic areas and hence produce the right principles for those products, out of which architectural requirements for these can be formulated. Once these are created, existing products can be compared to determine whether or not they match with these requirements.

Table 15 Balanced Score Card to elicit topic areas

| BSC Perspective | BSC Goal KPIs | Possible Topic Area per ITSA View ||||
		Business	Functional	Technical	Implementation
Customer	Return-business New customers	Loyalty programs	Sales channels Fulfillment processes	Customer data Security	
	Customer demographics or segments		Customer profile	Data warehouse	
	Purchase behavior (per demographic group)	Business Intelligence	Customer profile Customer ordering	Data warehouse Customer Data	Reporting process
	Bad debts	Customer handling	Customer profile	Customer data	Alert processes (who, what, when)
	Profitability by customer segment	Business Intelligence	Customer ordering	Data warehouse	Reporting process
	Alignment of customer requests and offerings	Customer handling	Process alignment	Process elements	Governance element usage
Processes	Number of activities	Value Chain	Process Efficiency		
	Opportunity success rate	Improvement loop		Business Technology Monitoring	Business Monitoring processes
	Accident ratios	Improvement loop		Business Technology Monitoring	Business Monitoring processes

Appendix B – The Balanced Score Card for Topic Areas

| BSC Perspective | BSC Goal KPIs | Possible Topic Area per ITSA View ||||
		Business	Functional	Technical	Implementation
	Equipment effectiveness,	Improvement loop		Business Technology Monitoring	Business Monitoring processes Product Selection
	Automated entry and approval	Value Chain	Process Efficiency	Customer Data	Product Selection
	Manual vs. IT-run processes	Process Efficiency	Process Services	Process Service Orchestration	Governance of services
Innovation	Investment Rate	Process priority		Business Technology Monitoring	Alert processes (who, what, when)
	Illness rate		Process support Workplace		Alert processes (who, what, when)
	Training effectiveness		Process descriptions	(Operational) Documentation	Process lifecycle Employee Training
	Employee		Self-help IT Support Process Support	(Operational) Documentation Helpdesk	Employee training
	Turnover	Improvement loop	Process Support		Alert processes (who, what, when)
Financial	cash flow days in payable days sales receivables	process efficiency	cost monitoring and reporting	business technology monitoring	reporting process
	market value add	value chain		process adaptability	

171

Appendix C – Sample Principle Statements

This Appendix contains some token principle statements that will only become proper principles when they have a rationale and have been reformulated to fit the organization's view on these issues. These statements are some of the many that have been collected by the authors over the years from books, articles, and client engagements and presented when examples of principle statements were asked. The origin or sources of these sample principle statements are lost in the mists of time.

We have made a division into two different parts: principle statements for organizations that do not have IT as their core business and those that do (outsourcing, managed services).

Organizations with No Core-IT Business

Business View

- Applications are driven from the business model.
- Information is managed according to our information policy as a corporate resource.
- Projects are financed based on a business case.
- It is the journey that matters, not the end-state.
  (Rationale: we don't know where we want to go, so decide step by step).
- Up-scaling is key for the solution.
  (Rationale: for commodity product large numbers must be possible without problems).
- Solution is beneficial for both parties.
  (Rationale: offer-you-cannot-refuse for consumer as well as producer).

Functional View

- We provide a consistent user experience even if the services are different and developed during a longer period of time.
- Physical location and structure of data are transparent to users.
- Data can be accessed concurrently.

Appendix C – Sample Principle Statements

- Applications are designed to execute in a global environment.
- Human factors are considered in all designs.
- There is corporate ownership of security definitions.
- Functions are reusable and reused.
- Single-sign-on covers application and all other services.
- Employee-facing services are provided in English first and additionally in local languages. Manager-facing services are provided in English only.
- The solution is the trusted single source of information.
- Usage metrics are captured automatically for services.
- User preferences can be customized for each user.
- Services can only be done in one way.

Technical View

- We employ reusable parts.
- Systems provide end-to-end management.
- We leverage existing assets.
- We are an early adopter of new technology.
- Data is captured at its source once, and then electronically distributed.
- The enterprise data model drives application architecture.
- Derivable data is not stored.
- Application security is based on predefined security levels and application category.
- Applications are designed in a layered architecture structure.
- Communication services are message-based through a single message standard.
- High usage distributed data must is cached at the customer.
- Business logic is present only in the workflow layer and not embedded in applications.

Appendix C – Sample Principle Statements

- Applications are opened up to allow atomic (logical) transactions.
- The content management is realized as a common solution.
- Industry standards are preferable to internal standards.

Implementation View

- Business driven development is governed by the content steering committee, design is based on authorised and mandated end user input.
- We execute our work in a manner to prevent problems rather than fix problems.
- A financing model for development initiatives is required.
- We prefer to buy IT components where market advantage is not a primary driver.
- All applications have a disaster recovery plan tailored to application category.
- A single standard development methodology is used.
- IT Architecture is controlled and maintained through architecture governance.
- Applications are maintained under version control.
- Application designs are modular.
- Quality improvement practices are employed across IT.

Organizations with Core-IT Business

Business View

- Exceptions to architectural principles, policies, and standards are documented and reviewed regularly as part of a comprehensive exception process.
- This IT Services Architecture is the authoritative source for best practices, policies, and standards in managed services delivery.
- As-is and to-be processes are defined prior to any service investments.

Appendix C – Sample Principle Statements

- A single process is used where business outcomes are essentially the same.
- Business process taxonomy drives creation and management of the architecture domains.

Functional View

- Business policy, including security policy, and all applicable laws are complied with in all operating regions impacted.
- All client business policy, including security policy, is complied with in all operating regions impacted for that client.
- Core business processes are maintained end-to-end as a company-wide asset, and they define value delivery chains around a total customer experience.
- Intended impact and potential unintended impact (risk) to the business are clearly documented, with assumptions credibly justified.
- Customer data quality is owned by the customer.

Technical View

- Data has a definitive source and ownership. Customer data is a customer corporate asset.
- Enterprise data models are based on those purchased with core applications, and are used and reused by all applications.
- Enterprise standard data definitions are used and reused by all applications.
- Compartmentalization of customer data drives overall data architecture.
- Alignment with industry standards facilitates interoperability among disparate infrastructures, applications, and data across the enterprise. Applications use inter-application interfaces that tend toward industry-standard real-time messaging technology.
- Reuse, reduce, consolidate, and share globally - Existing solutions are reused instead of building new ones, even if it means giving up minor functionality. Applications are consolidated and shared where possible, and types, versions, and instances are reduced across customers and geographies.

Appendix C – Sample Principle Statements

- Products of our strategic alliance partners are utilized wherever and whenever possible to leverage existing support structures, improve products, and drive down unit delivery costs.

- Metrics are defined and implemented at the appropriate level.

- Information system boundaries are clearly defined and documented, as are their linkages with other information systems.

- Infrastructure solutions are scalable, have high performance, and are capable of supporting volatile workloads.

- The IT Services architecture supports solutions that manage and control IT services and infrastructure using automation wherever possible.

- Business rules are implemented as policies that control automated processes.

- Business and operational metrics are collected, aggregated, and summarized as appropriate, and are made available to automation processes on demand.

Implementation View

- We drive simplification to reduce complexity.

- Capacity is managed across the IT infrastructure worldwide to maximize service delivery efficiencies.

- Deployments scale using the smallest practical number of instances, are capable of supporting volatile workloads, and can support multiple customers and multiple geographic regions across the globe.

- Processes required for deployment lifecycle support are considered before investing in any new implementations.

- Implementations and upgrades of infrastructure, services, or solutions, have a minimal effect on our customer's business.

- Repetitive processes prone to human error are automated, and are triggered by IT events in a closed-loop system.

Appendix D – Tool Bag

This appendix contains a number of templates that can used in architectural engagements to extract or document architectural choices expressed by the client, based on the HPGM for ITSA methodology. For the specifics about the type of content to fill in, refer to the chapters of this book that cover the ITSA framework elements.

Principles Capture Template

Capturing the architectural principles in any of the four ITSA views, as expressed in initial and follow-on stakeholder meetings, is important because it represents one of the fundamental ingredients of the architecture. Tools and electronic processing of these principles are useful but often not the right choice during the principles defining and elicitation process. Below, there is a template to enter the information on the spot. This may be done either by jotting down the information using paper and pen or by typing in this information in an electronic template.

Business Drivers

Driver ID	Driver Description
BD1	description
BD2	
BDn	

Business Goals

Goal ID	Goal Description	Goal metrics
BG1	description	Metric
BG2		
BGn		

Appendix D – Tool Bag

Business Principles

Principle ID	Topic Area	Principle statement	Rationales	Implications	Obstacles
BP1			BGn	implication implication	obstacle obstacle
BP2					
BPn					

Actions by Implications (Tasks)

Implication	Action	By When	By Whom
1			
2			

Actions by Obstacles (Risks)

Obstacle	Action	By When	By Whom
1			
2			

Appendix D – Tool Bag

Functional Principles

Principle ID	Topic Area	Principle statement	Rationales	Implications	Obstacles
FP1			BGn	implication	obstacle
			BPn	implication	obstacle
FP2					
FPn					

Actions by Implications (Tasks)

Implication	Action	By When	By Whom
1			
2			

Actions by Obstacles (Risks)

Obstacle	Action	By When	By Whom
1			
2			

Appendix D – Tool Bag

Technical Principles

Principle ID	Topic Area	Principle statement	Rationales	Implications	Obstacles
TP1			BGn	implication	obstacle
			BPn	implication	obstacle
			FPn		
TP2					
TPn					

Actions by Implications (Tasks)

Implication	Action	By When	By Whom
1			
2			

Actions by Obstacles (Risks)

Obstacle	Action	By When	By Whom
1			
2			

Appendix D – Tool Bag

Implementation Principles

Principle ID	Topic Area	Principle statement	Rationales	Implications	Obstacles
IP1			BGn	implication	obstacle
			BPn	implication	obstacle
			FPn		
			TPn		
IP2					
IPn					

Actions by Implications (Tasks)

Implication	Action	By When	By Whom
1			
2			

Actions by Obstacles (Risks)

Obstacle	Action	By When	By Whom
1			
2			

Appendix D – Tool Bag

Requirements Capture Template

Requirements that are elicited and defined during the architecture blueprint process as elements of each ITSA view are identified by attributes that are best summarized in a template such as the one below.

Business Requirements

Requirement ID:	BR<nn>
Specification:	
Justification:	
Source:	
Impact:	
Issues:	
Related requirements:	

Functional Requirements

Requirement ID:	FR<nn>
Specification:	
Justification:	
Source:	
Impact:	
Issues:	
Related requirements:	

Technical Requirements

Requirement ID:	TR<nn>
Specification:	
Justification:	
Source:	
Impact:	
Issues:	
Related requirements:	

Appendix D – Tool Bag

Implementation Requirements

Requirement ID:	IR<nn>
Specification:	
Justification:	
Source:	
Impact:	
Issues:	
Related requirements:	

Appendix D – Tool Bag

Model Capture Template

Models defined as elements of an ITSA view are identified by attributes that are best summarized in a template such as the one below. This summary becomes part of the model itself (as capture box).

Business Models

Model ID:	BM<nn>
Purpose:	
Related to:	
Legend:	
Timeline:	
Description:	

Functional Models

Model ID:	FM<nn>
Purpose:	
Related to:	
Legend:	
Timeline:	
Description:	

Technical Models

Model ID:	TM<nn>
Purpose:	
Related to:	
Legend:	
Timeline:	
Description:	

Appendix D – Tool Bag

Implementation Models

Model ID:	IM<nn>
Purpose:	
Related to:	
Legend:	
Timeline:	
Description:	

Appendix E – Case Study: Information Worker 2.0

It is almost a cliché to mention that the information age has a tremendous impact on our society, but we do see fundamental changes in information intensive organizations. Information technology is intertwined with their operations and through innovative IT concepts; workers are able to work in almost any location and empowered to act anytime anywhere. The traditional fixed work place in an office is rapidly losing its importance in favor of a more fluid, less centralized work model. Where information was compartmentalized in the past, these dividing walls now disappear (thanks to IT) and open up new opportunities. Even the location is no longer fixed with the arrival of the Internet and wireless connectivity to it in many places – from clients via conference centers, coffee shops to home.

A current trend we see is the introduction of another way of working that tries to cope with this fluid working model; a style we call in this case study 'Information Worker 2.0,' or IW2.0 for short. The separation between office hours and private time is no longer clear, and a new way of working is emerging.[67]

In the following sections, we will highlight a small subset of an architecture engagement for a large institution that wants to adopt the IW2.0 approach. This example illustrates some highlights of the ITSA views and their elements in this engagement. For this reason the example is incomplete on purpose. Any other organization going for IW2.0 will have its own architecture, fitted to its own situation.

The IT component is only one of the three major pillars supporting IW2.0, and we have seen all three before as ITSA implication aspects:

- People – the employee: organization, culture, mentality
- Process – the work environment: physical locations and infrastructure
- Technology – virtual locations through IT platforms, components, devices, office automation

---

[67] See for example http://www.microsoft.com/southafrica/office/new_world.mspx

Appendix E – Case Study: Information Worker 2.0

The Case

The organization that wants to introduce IW2.0 is a large bank with many offices, where clients are assisted with normal bank transactions but also with larger financial investment consultancy or advice on stock portfolio. Employees visit clients to provide consultancy on their premises, but need to connect to back-office systems in the office to complete their work. Clients can also perform a number of self-help operations via the web interface of the bank.

The bank wants to cut down on operational expenditures by exploiting the new opportunities present in IT today to shift administrative burdens towards the employee. This involves more responsibility on the part of the employees – making them self supporting. This also implies that employees must be able to work from various locations and in different time frames, singly or as part of their group. In summary, the bank wants to make work efforts more flexible and more tailored to the employees' work and lifestyle. What needs to be done to implement IW2.0 such that it fits the bank's culture and capabilities?

Business Drivers and Goals

An initial SWOT analysis was performed to make it more explicit what strengths, weaknesses, and threats presented themselves and how they can be used to identify and realize opportunities to the bank.

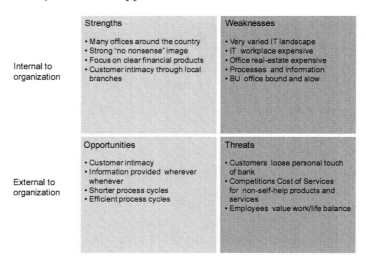

Figure 45: Strength/Weakness analysis

Appendix E – Case Study: Information Worker 2.0

From the SWOT analysis, a number of business drivers and goals were formulated. Drivers (pain, regulatory, or opportunity) that force the bank to change its current position find their root in the weaknesses and threats. The following drivers were identified:

Driver ID	Driver Description
BD1	Old office-based approach loses business opportunities
BD2	Operational spending is too high

Goals derived from this SWOT and using the strengths of the bank are identified as:

Goal ID	Goal Description	Goal Metrics
BG1	Introduce Information Worker 2.0 (IW2.0) throughout the bank	Within two years
BG2	Reduction of work place expenditures	By 10% one year after introduction of IW2.0

Topic Areas

Areas for decisions and important directions of the solution are defined as topic areas. These can be deduced from the SWOT results and/or Balanced Score Card set initiatives and their KPIs (key performance metrics). Figure 46 shows a set of topic areas to cover.

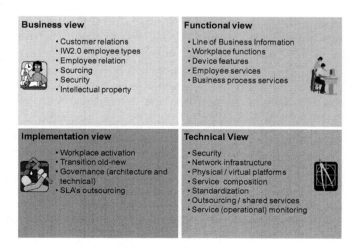

Figure 46: Topic areas applied in each view

Appendix E – Case Study: Information Worker 2.0

The business view focuses on why the bank thinks it adds value to its clients and employees, and in what areas firm decisions are needed to facilitate this. For example within 'customer relations' some principles can be developed to define what services are affected, which will be bound to a particular location, and which ones can be provided from more or any location. The implications will then list what is needed to make this possible. The 'IW2.0 employee types' topic area will lead to decisions on what types of workers (and why) make up the bank population and have different needs and opportunities regarding the IW2.0 environment. 'Sourcing' is important to define why certain IT aspects remain core to the bank while others can be left to third parties. For example, depending on the conditions, we choose whether we want certain activities to be handled in-house, offshore, or if we want to completely outsource them.

In the functional view, it is important to decide what type of information the users need to perform their job. This differs among the various types of desk-bound users, but even more so for people without a fixed workplace. 'Workplace Functions' requires decisions on the configuration of each IW2.0 type worker's workplace, his communication devices, display and input devices, etc. 'Employee services' typically invites principles on services the employees need to support their administrative tasks like agenda management, conference room booking, travel arrangements, etc.

In the technical view, decisions are needed on how the IW2.0 is realized. 'Security' is an obvious area for situations where information goes beyond the bank building boundaries, not only for connections and transport of information but also for the storage of it in case local copies are held on personal devices (which may get lost). The 'Network infrastructure' is needed to define how workers connect to their work IT environment safely and always as expected. Availability and reliability will be important issues here. 'Service composition' taps into the functional view 'business process services' with decisions supporting the simplification of services and shorter time to market goals. 'Service (operational) monitoring' is the internal aspect of ensuring how reliable and predictable those services are, and whether the bank wants to proactively repair potential failure situations or increase capacity on demand.

In the implementation view, the governance of the total architecture (of which the IT part is only a part, as we explained earlier) as well as the IT specific part needs to be well guarded and nourished when new demands and insights need to find a place in the (un)modified architecture. 'Workplace activation' and 'Transition old-new' are about how new services for employees are granted and how the old situation is converted into the new one.

Appendix E – Case Study: Information Worker 2.0

Business View

Business Principles

Based on the business view topic areas, a number of principles are defined to fit the bank. Each of them must support the business goals while their content is inspired by the topic area. We only provide a few sample principles here and carry them through into the subsequent views, where supporting principles are defined. This demonstrates the seamless chain of justification through the rationale – an aspect that ensures we only do what directly supports the business goals. We will leave out the actions and assignments to people.

Principle ID	Topic Area	Principle statement	Rationales	Implications	Obstacles
BP01	Customer relations	Customer services are delivered at client preferred locations	BG1	Employees can access core applications from remote locations Employees have portable devices to access information A secure infrastructure allows access by remote worker Application data is centrally stored and online updated (one version of the truth)	Remote network access unavailable
BP02	Sourcing	IT facilities are outsourced	BG2	IT provider complies with bank regulations (Sarbanes-Oxley, privacy, Basel II, etc.) IT governance structure operational	IT provider cannot provide audit information for regulations
BP03	IW2.0 types	Workplace functionality is demand driven by business units (hence its users)	BG1	Business user groups and roles are defined based on their work type Work scenarios for each group or role are driven System interactions are tailored to work scenarios and device types (GUI's etc.)	Potentially too many different user groups Problem defining tailoring within a single group

Appendix E – Case Study: Information Worker 2.0

Business Model

Because not all employees of the bank are equal, a subdivision is made to categorize them into four different types, all differently impacted by the IW2.0 solution. The division into four groups came after a discussion of what distinguishes one type of employees from another. Figure 47 shows a model from the business view where we see along the vertical axis, whether work requires office presence or can be performed at any place and is mobile. The horizontal axis is whether a person works independently or is part of a team and works on a community effort.

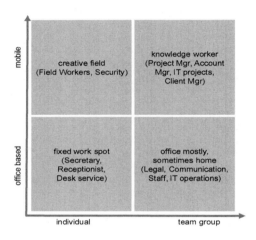

Figure 47: Type of workers

Different solutions of the IW2.0 are needed to fit each category. This must be investigated and elaborated on.

Appendix E – Case Study: Information Worker 2.0

Functional View

Based on the business view, a number of functional principles can be defined to support the business goals, drivers, and principles. The functional topic areas provide inspiration or guidance to create functional principles. Below, we show only a few principles that are essential to the IW2.0 solution stated in this case, including a functional model. They are linked to the business view as shown above, and demonstrate the chain of justification through the rationales.

Functional Principles

Principle ID	Topic Area	Principle statement	Rationales	Implications	Obstacles
FP01	Workplace features	Mobile workers perform core processes online	BG1 BP1	Secure connection with infrastructure present Offline work limited to non-core processes Alternative communication channel available (fallback)	Network providers do not provide 100% coverage
FP02	Employee services	Employees are self supporting regarding administrative tasks	BG1 BG2 BP01	Self-service portal in place to provide calendar, expenses, meeting room, travel, etc. Workforce transformation to IW2.0	Some administrative systems may not be suitable for self service (portal) environment
FP03	Workplace features	Workplace functionality based on worker scenarios	BP03	User types defined Scenarios for each type defined User/system interface on each scenario defined	

Functional Model

Each worker needs different functionality to perform his job properly. The characteristics of the work and the implied needs define the functionality required for the four defined types of workplaces for the same number of worker types. This is shows in the functional model in Figure 48.

Appendix E – Case Study: Information Worker 2.0

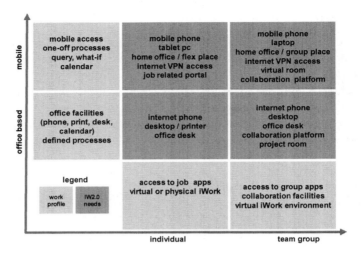

Figure 48: Types of workplace functionality for worker types

Appendix E – Case Study: Information Worker 2.0

Technical View

Based on the functional view, a number of techniques can be defined that facilitate the IW2.0 solution. As with previous sections of this case, we only show a few technical principles that are key to the IW2.0 solution.

Technical Principles

Principle ID	Topic Area	Principle statement	Rationales	Implications	Obstacles
TP01	Physical/virtual platform	Employee workplaces are virtualized with limited offline work for non-core processes	BG2	Core applications only available online Collaboration items can be stored/worked on locally but are synch-ed during connection Work environment performance stable due to scaling Centralized single sign-on and access security	Vital apps unavailable with network problems All workplaces unavailable with infrastructure problems
TP02	Security	Remote access to infrastructure limited to VPN connections	BG1 BP01	Access security model defined ActiveCard for each user Security model on user/application in operation and audit-logged	
TP03	Network infrastructure	Infrastructure allows for flexible work times	BG1 BP01 FP03	Infrastructure continuity measures for prolonged support (HW, SW, service hours) in place Fallback scenario allows for multiple entry points into infrastructure	

Technical Model

With different types of users, each user has his or her own virtual workspace. This workspace is based on one of the four templates (defined for each type of user), which will run on a physical server destined for virtual workspace support.

Appendix E – Case Study: Information Worker 2.0

Similarly, application and database servers (as well as other types) are all modeled on specialized templates for virtual servers configured to support their contents optimally. Figure 49 depicts this technique in the technical model.

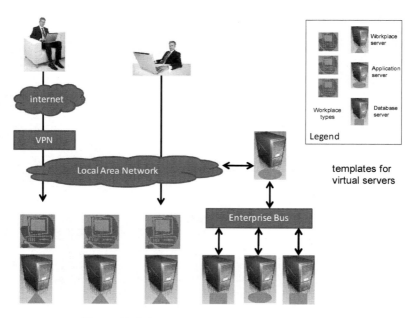

Figure 49: Information Worker 2.0 technical model

Appendix E – Case Study: Information Worker 2.0

Implementation View

Implementation Principles

Principle ID	Topic Area	Principle statement	Rationales	Implications	Obstacles
IP01	Transition	Business units lead the workplace design and implementation	BP3	Visualization and business unit scenarios are defined before any workplace is created	Complexity in work scenarios might hinder a common solution
IP02	Transition	Delivery of new workplace for all users of one type at same time regardless location	BP03 FP03	All systems for a user type have been workplace enabled All users have been trained in new workplace functionality and process All users have new, identical devices for work (standardization) Transition of (work) data from old personal device to central location completed prior to transition	Complexity with apps used by different user types Investment in new equipment

Typical models for the implementation view could be, for example, a Gantt chart that prioritizes business units for the transformation process work break down structures, or a division of responsibilities that can include a sourcing organization, or vendor, etc.

Appendix F – HPGM for ITSA, the Journey

A narrative by Rob Kruijk

Spring 1995. I get a call from the European HQ of Digital Equipment Corporation, from the Head of Consulting Services, and he asks me if I can create a real architecture method from the various approaches that are running about in the organization. He adds 'before it is too late.' This is because since about 5 years Digital is downsizing substantially and we want to prevent losing knowledge and experience about architecture-like work. I get a mandate with the funds to organize and develop things.

The first step is a meeting with representatives from key geographies to see what is left in terms of knowledge, methods, and materials, but also what the market potential is for an architecture kind of approach to solving IT problems. We are inspired by a method called DART. DART stands for Digital Architecture Response Teams and is based on PRISM, a piece of practical research done by CSC Index, Inc. and Hammer and Company, Inc. sponsored by vendors such as Digital Equipment Corporation. Mike Hammer is a prominent figure in that work. DART had been introduced to us in The Netherlands in the early nineties during a so-called Summer School for consultants. But, apart from talking about it with clients, we had not done a real client engagement with it. Elsewhere in Europe, but also in the US this is not really taking off too.

With Peter Haynes, an experienced consultant from the UK who had just left Digital, I continue this work and we are able to track down the material we still have and create a usable and sellable method. In 1995 we spend a couple of weeks together in the Digital Equipment office in Utrecht, the Netherlands. Peter and I develop a shared vision on the key values of the fundamentals that constitute DART:

- Distinct domains of the architecture – business, systems, technical and product architecture domain.
- The use of principles across the views as the core fabric of the architecture, based on the principle statement itself with the added power of consistently using the attributes of rationale, implications, and obstacles.
- The use of models to create oversight, to visualize principles, and to show coherence, connections, and dependencies.
- The ability to use and position standards.

Appendix F – HPGM for ITSA, the Journey

Based on this, a very effective and companionable collaboration develops. We collect materials and, in doing so, the approach emerges to use 'training' as the first form of a deliverable to get things going. This has turned out to be very fundamental. We could have taken the course to publish a method and then get it approved, etc. But that would, undoubtedly, have gotten us into a 'method debate,' with all the risks thereof. What unfolded was an 'organic' rather than an 'organizational' way and this has been the approach ever since. Looking at this in hindsight, I can see the following benefits:

- Get the (potential) practitioners involved right away.
    - Immediate feedback and contributions for method enhancement
    - Start of a 'ground swell' community
- Create management visibility in a practical way, through their people.

The second fundamental decision was to the make the training case-based, with participants having to act as the client with a problem or opportunity to be tackled with this method. In other words: course participants would get trained in the method by undergoing it as a user. Hence, we developed a case and the materials, proposed a course (3 days, I believe), got it approved, got a quorum of participants, and launched the premiere in September 1995.

But, in parallel, other things evolved. During a trip to the US for another purpose in August, I connect to an emerging corporate program within Digital Equipment called 'Solution Architecture,' I make contact with the corporate part of that community and manage to get approval for a workshop in the US on solution architecture with key players from the US (Corporate and Field) and Europe, facilitated by Peter Haynes and using the emerging architecture method on the question: why should Digital Equipment care about Solution Architecture?

So, from here on a momentum is created along different, but coherent paths in the latter part of 1995:

- Training was developed and delivered
- Corporate strategy workshop about whether solution architecture is beneficial
- And, last but most certainly not least, the first use in a client situation.

It is the third one that gave the biggest impulse for changes to the DART method which should be mentioned before developing the first two paths

Appendix F – HPGM for ITSA, the Journey

further, as this all happened in the September-November 1995 timeframe. Two major changes are made to DART:

- The (four) architecture domains are renamed to views.
- The views are associated with business, functional, technical, and implementation aspects.

This means that we now have a basic architecture framework consisting of business view, functional view, technical view, and implementation view. In retrospect, this happened quite intuitively. As far as I can remember, the basic motivation for adopting views was (a) to make the model less technical, with a greater business and organizational orientation, and (b) to talk to non-technical people, the word 'view' is less intimidating than 'architecture.' In line with this increased business orientation, the elements 'business drivers' and business goals' – including metrics – are added to the business view.

> **1995** My first real architecture workshop at the Dutch Social Security Agency. The scope is management information for steering and measuring the business with a Data Warehouse solution. Twenty people participate in a two-day workshop, among whom are several senior business managers. I come up with the concept of 'business driver' on the spot and this brings out a major discrepancy in thinking between business managers, which the architecture process is able to solve very well. The workshop results in a useful conceptual architecture of the intended solution which gets the project off to a good start.

In spite of having been thrown into the deep end, thanks to the help of a good Digital team (two consultants and a project manager), this worked out well and yields invaluable learning points, most significantly the notion that our four views, in fact, are stakeholder views, and we start to position them as follows:

- The business view represents the business sponsor and answers the 'why' question.
- The functional view represents the business user and answers the 'what' question.
- The technical view represents the builder (of the solution) and answers the 'how' question.
- The implementation view represents the operator and answers the 'with' question.

Appendix F – HPGM for ITSA, the Journey

Moreover, the first two views together express 'desirability,' whereas the second two views express 'do ability' of the intended solution. These things turn out to be vitally important for 'marketing' the whole solution architecture concept, both within Digital – consultants, people who are calling themselves (solution) architect, sales people, managers, etc. – as well as with clients. It certainly helps the other two paths unfolding at the same time – the training and the Corporate SA Strategy workshop.

The training path (Europe)

The first training is held in the Digital Equipment office in Utrecht, The Netherlands, in September 1995. Peter Haynes and I are the instructors and in attendance are about 10 students from different countries. As with the first client workshop, the 'givers' learn as much, if not more, than the 'takers.' The course gets a good rating from the participants and we are encouraged (and also given permission) to organize a second one, incorporating all the things learned during the first one. BUT, much to our surprise, we do not get enough student enrollments and we have to cancel the course. It turned out that we needed a hot case that really demonstrates the connection with field reality, to make people enroll for this course.

The strategy path (Corporate)

Meanwhile, the Corporate Strategy workshop on solution architecture is held in the United States at the Digital HQ in the Spitbrook facilities in Nashua (NH), and is a great success. Well-attended by 10-15 people, with a good mix of Corporate and Field, it covers a lot of ground. Peter Haynes does an excellent job as a facilitator (so I can be a participant) and we gather a coherent set of ideas to put solution architecture on the map. The main outcomes lead to two important initiatives after a few months:

- The creation of an Architecture Program Office (APO)
- A new name for the transformed DART: DSAT – Digital Solution Architecture Technique; we call it 'technique' rather than 'method' because we feel that we need the ecosystem of community of practitioners, developed and re-used collateral, standard training, etc. to get to a full-fledged method.

But training funds for further development are not readily available and the training effort in Europe is stalled. We find ourselves presented with the blocking of the organic growth path that we had chosen – without training, no practitioners and without practitioners, no architecture.

In The Netherlands we then take another breakthrough (retrospect) decision in November (still) 1995. The solution architecture training must be

Appendix F – HPGM for ITSA, the Journey

based on an IT theme that is hot. We considered using the data warehouse case from the Dutch Social Security Agency as this seemed a hot IT topic. For educational purposes however, this case turned out to be too complicated and we diverted to another data warehouse case from a presales situation with a mobile phone operator in Germany delivered by the same team from Digital Equipment that engaged with the Social Security Agency. The case is going to be called MPC – Mobile Phone Company. So we have a hot IT topic in a hot emerging business. The first run of this course is done in The Netherlands in February 1996 and we have 16 participants in no time, and even a waiting list with people from all over Europe. This already being 'just what the doctor ordered,' when I tell the people of the emerging architecture program office in the United States about this, they want to send two people over to evaluate the course.

The case works well and the four teams work hard to develop an initial solution architecture using the DSAT framework. They all present their result at the end and there is a little competition to award the best team. Our US observers are impressed and they write a favorable review with very good pointers for improvement. The key message is that the course is taken on board in the US (Corporate and Field) as an official one, with no course development needed. The training is given three times in the US, in Detroit (MI), Nashua (NH), and Irvine (CA) in the course of 1996/7.

In the same period there are several more in Europe and also one in Tokyo, with help from the Corporate Data Warehousing Team. It is striking how serious the Japanese organization picks this up and it shows later on.

1996 At a Polish mobile operator in Warsaw we get a chance to do a case just like our course case. The main emphasis is marketing information. Because they are in the middle of starting up a major campaign, people are moving in and out of the workshop. But we manage to just proceed with the process and again the business participation is great. This case, and many thereafter, shows the strength of the process based 'on separation, yet traceability of concern.' That keeps things going in a meaningful way, in spite of varying people participating. We manage to bring to bear many tradeoffs on the business-IT knife's edge. I vividly remember that a lady from Marketing decided to attend the technical view session. When an IT person suggested that 'this or that is also possible,' she said: 'No, I don't want my people to be able to do that.'

All these developments quickly lead to the creation of a group of 150-200 trained people, who not all become practicing architects, because there is

Appendix F – HPGM for ITSA, the Journey

more to that than just training, but it sure is the beginning of a community of architects.

So, two years after the beginning of this effort, we are well underway. Our DSAT framework is well established and is developing into a method. The emerging program office develops into a true Architecture Program Office (APO) with another key person coming on board to lead it: Leo Laverdure, who has a vast software engineering (management) experience and a good feel for architecture. Management support is now strong to the extent of funding for training and the APO, but getting the architecture-led approach established in the consultancy and projects business is going very slowly. However, we boldly propose to organize a World Wide Architecture meeting called ArchitectureWorks. This proposal is accepted and we stage the first one in Nashua NH, in the beginning of 1997.

ArchitetectureWorks is significant because by selected management and Human Resources (HR) department's participation, the start is made to formalize the solution architect role into a new job category. Also, the name DSAT (Digital Solution Architecture Technique) is formalized. The most important thing, however, is that practitioners can talk to practitioners, the mark of a true community of practice. This is very motivating and brings out the strengths of our approach. People are using it for all sorts of solutions in all industries and that is very good to see.

The change from Digital Equipment to Compaq Computers in the first half of 1998 does not stop the bandwagon. On the contrary, changing the name from DSAT to CSAM (Compaq Solution Architecture Method) signifies (a) that Compaq takes it on board as a brand and (b) that we are now confident enough to call it a methodology. We can start to be serious about collateral and continue to drive training as a major engine for expanding the community and using the method.

A major new step in the way we do training is the development of the so-called Delivery Training. This is a 5-day intensive training where 4 groups each act as facilitators for one of the architecture views while the others role-play the client audience. The case developed for this is WorkSpace, an office furniture manufacturer who 'goes on the Web.' Leo Laverdure and I develop the course and also teach the first run. As we embark on this new training plateau, we have to beef up our capacity to deliver what are now two basis courses: CSAM Introduction and CSAM Delivery. All the courses so far have claimed very good student ratings and it is very important that we keep that up. The APO is getting well-staffed up to 4 professionals to further evolve the methodology, develop collateral and essential training material. The US based APO naturally takes care of the Americas, and where needed the Far East, while in Europe we rely on the early adopters.

Appendix F – HPGM for ITSA, the Journey

> **1999** A very large scale email project at an international large scale bank is running into problems in a design and build phase mix-up. The four CSAM views are used as a diagnostic instrument to separate design from development by creating architecture principles, which shows clearly that not having those in the first place gets you into trouble.

In the new Compaq environment CSAM blossoms and is taken on board by the young Compaq-heritage sales force quite well. One token of this is the fact that CSAM training features in the high-powered eBusiness University in 1999. International architecture universities continue with one more in the US and three in Europe, with the last one in November 2005.

Entering the new millennium, I get the opportunity to visit China in various places (Hong Kong, Sjanghai, Beijing and Fuzhou) and do about 10 client workshops with the help of Cecia Wong, which puts CSAM very much on the map with Cecia as a leading architect and instructor for years to come. Later on, I do major client engagements in South Africa, Malaysia, Sweden, Finland, Denmark, Italy, UK, and Northern Ireland.

> **2001** Two cases stand out for me in the work in China.
>
> One is a large workshop with delegates from seven Western China Provinces plus a few Compaq partners, which created an architectural concept for an e-Commerce Strategy for all seven of them, plus a collaborative approach put in the form of the West China e-Commerce Alliance – all in two days.
>
> The other is a small workshop with the management team of a small hosting service provider with a huge investment capital behind it to create the largest Integrated Data Service Center in China. CSAM proved very useful to put this vision into a reasonably thought-out model to scale up very rapidly.

In 2002, there is another main event – the merger of Compaq with Hewlett-Packard (HP). This poses a new challenge for the methodology. Whereas Compaq did not have a services division, choice of services methodologies from Digital Equipment wasn't at stake. HP does have one, so the question is if CSAM will be accepted. The answer is a clear 'yes' and a substantial and successful effort is expended to have CSAM get the HP Global Method label, but is renamed to HPGM for IT Strategy & Architecture (HPGM for ITSA). Leo Laverdure is instrumental in this.

Appendix F – HPGM for ITSA, the Journey

In a big training program, hundreds of pre-merger HP people are being trained in a now fully established architecture profession with around 1800 members. Meanwhile, around 2005 the Leadership of the APO is taken over by Len Fehskens, who had joined the APO with a strong architecture background in engineering. I especially remember his work in Digital Network Architecture (DNA) in the mid-eighties. Before taking on the APO Leadership, Len was the driving and content-creating force in extending HPGM for ITSA with a blueprinting method. So we now have ITSA Concept and ITSA Blueprint Architectures. Blueprints extend the causality of the Solution Concept towards feasible solution designs based on precisely developed requirements. Peter Beijer in the Netherlands was (one of) the first architect(s) to do real Blueprint development work in 2001.

2003 At a world-wide logistics operator, based in Copenhagen, we practically 'steal' this engagement from the hands of the incumbent vendor. By a very successful ITSA workshop we were able to quickly create an architectural concept for their business need to automate the workflow of their container-shipping business. Based on this, we manage to 'sell-through' a large ITSA Blueprint development engagement based on Peter Beijer's example. The Danish team does an exceptionally good job here. This is also a shining example of the effectiveness of knowledge transfer using architecture.

2004 A global supplier in telecommunications, based in Stockholm. This is a very special case because the client's two outsourcing partners both participate in a two-day ITSA workshop with the client. The scope is also special – a much more formal and manageable segmentation of the development and production environments of the business of building telephone exchanges. Besides the outcome of the workshop giving a very useful direction for moving forward, the client is very pleased with the positive and close collaboration between the two incumbent outsourcing providers created by putting them through this architecture process.

From 2006 on, the architecture horizon is extended to the enterprise scope. An attempt is made to develop an enterprise architecture (EA) method, but that effort does not reach beyond recommending the HP-IT 'pyramid' model with the layers of strategy, processes, information, applications, application infrastructure, and core infrastructure. In my last year before retirement in April 2007, I experiment with some success with transforming key principles and models from major (i.e. large scope like programs) ITSA engagements into enterprise principles in whatever model

Appendix F – HPGM for ITSA, the Journey

the client prefers. This can be called 'EA through the back door,' a bottom-up and evolutionary alternative to large-scale EA efforts.

> **2006** Northern Ireland Civil Service. Large effort, extremely well picked up by the client, to create both an (ITSA) Architecture Concept plus ensuing Architecture Blueprint for the Shared Services Center consolidating NICS' entire IT infrastructure. This causes a successful first-phase implementation in 2007 for which, in the words of the Program Manager who also plays the role of Design Authority (and very well too), the extensive use of architecture was indispensable.

This leads to the development of reference architectures for large initiatives in the Workplace, e-Government, and Enterprise Information Management areas, thus creating a very insightful so-called Reference Architecture Library in 2009.

We have come a long way since 1995, when we first started to adapt the DART adopted PRISM approach into a Solution Architecture approach. This is remarkable, as PRISM was the first enterprise architecture approach back in 1985 and we are now applying HPGM for ITSA to create enterprise architectures, either through the 'back door' or to develop, for example, TOGAF based enterprise architectures.

Overseeing all this, which is the great opportunity of having written this narrative, these seem to have been the directions, turning points, creative insights, etc. which have made a difference:

- Using what's there. We have started from PRISM, which we intuitively liked, first and foremost the linkable principles by their attributes of rationale, implications, and obstacles.

- Going for solution architecture, even while starting with a method that inherently was enterprise-oriented.

- Adapt what you start with by real-life use and education. This forces you to be practical and good.

- Creating status by training practitioners as though they were users, by case-based training, letting them go through what their clients would go through when they would do it to them. Many a time a client would ask after a workshop: 'Do you have a course for this?' To which the answer was: 'You just had one.'

Appendix F – HPGM for ITSA, the Journey

- Making the views of the architecture model stakeholder views. This made the method accessible to business people.

- Creating two levels of architectural granularity: Concept and Blueprint, with the Blueprint providing the connection with the IT solution design process.

- Use the method with an open mind – for diagnostic besides just design purposes, for reference architectures, as for project as well as program architectures, as straw man enterprise architectures, etc., to any kind of business problem or opportunity, in any industry and in a variety of cultures.

- Forever refine both the education and the method itself and enlarge and enrich the body of knowledge.

- Be aware that architecture is the best knowledge (and experience) management system (and process), and use it that way.

I am aware that hindsight is 20/20 vision, but the value of overseeing things in this way brings up a number of things that are pretty useful for introducing serious IT Architecture practices in any business or organization. In line with the nine points above, the following people have contributed largely to this story:

- Peter Haynes, who helped to salvage materials from obsolescence and put the training together in the beginning and later on became our 'master teacher'

- Hennie Olthof, who as a domain expert was instrumental in putting the first major course 'Solution Architecture Data Warehousing' together and teaching it

- Scott Crowther played a key role in putting SA-training in Corporate training programs and helped create the first World wide ArchitectureWorks conference

- Leo Laverdure, who built up the Architecture Program Office (APO), bringing in and leading people like:
    o Pat Srite for admin/logistics and knowledge management support; she became the 'mother of the architect profession'
    o Larry Sojda as a major practitioner and trainer in the US
    o Alex Conn as a major practitioner, who together with Leo, formalized and extended the CSAM methodology. He

Appendix F – HPGM for ITSA, the Journey

> created the Service Delivery Kit and numerous training materials
>> o Kristin Rounds, who played a major role in course development

- Cecia Wong was a major practitioner and trainer in the Far East
- Theo de Klerk for delivering and further evolving ITSA trainings
- Len Fehskens, who created the Blueprint part of ITSA and led the APO and, indeed, HP towards a major contributor and user of the Open Group standards effort with respect to method and practitioner certification

Indeed we have come a long way...

Rob Kruijk, Abcoude, October 2009

About the Authors

Peter Beijer – over 30 years experience in IT, practicing IT architecture since 1997. Enterprise Architect in Hewlett-Packard's (HP) Enterprise Services organization and architecture profession lead for HP in the Netherlands. He is a recognized pioneer in practicing HP's Solution Architecture Blueprinting methodology and a core contributor to the development of the architecture profession, where he also is a frequent instructor and developer of HP's IT architecture methodology course collateral. He participates in the IT governance working group of the Netherlands Architecture Forum. He is a member of the Open Group IT Architecture Certification (ITAC) Specification Authority that defines and maintains ITAC certification criteria, serves as eligible certification board member and chair, and is certified by the Open Group as Master Certified IT Architect. He received a Master's degree in information management, Cum Laude, from the University of Amsterdam. He is a research fellow and Ph.D. candidate of PrimaVera, the research programme on information management at the University of Amsterdam.

Theo de Klerk – with 30 years of IT experience, practicing IT architecture since 1999 as Solution Architect at Hewlett-Packard's (HP) Consulting & Integration organization on various areas involving system integration and business technology optimization. Started at Digital Equipment's Educational Services in 1980 as instructor and course developer. Later moved to Software & Application Services, designing and developing custom-specified systems. He was lead assessor guiding Compaq to ISO9001 certification in 1992, after which he turned to distributed system integration architecture based on Forté and Microsoft technologies. During this effort, he became involved in applying and later instructing HP IT architecture methodology within HP-led projects and contributed to the maturing process of this methodology and its curriculum. Certified by the Open Group as Master Certified IT Architect. Coach for candidates aspiring to ITAC certification. Eligible ITAC certification board member. Frequent publisher of HP internal architecture papers and webinars. He holds an M.Sc. degree in physics and mathematics from the University of Amsterdam with a minor in astronomy. He has a keen interest in pure science education, astronomy, and cosmology.

Index

agility, 51
alignment, 5, 6, 130
applications, 16
architect
    acountability, 145
    blends, 150
    career path, 149
    certification, 151
    role, 8, 49, 129, 136, 140, 148
    skills, 144
architectural view, 30
architecture blueprint, 6, 32, 33, 110, 115, 120, 122, 123, 133
architecture concept, 32, 109, 121, 123, 133
ASL, 131
Balanced Score Card, 42, 89, 161, 162, 165, 169, 191
Basel II, 37, 68
BiSL, 131
BPR, 4
business drivers, 31, 32, 35, 36, 38, 42, 45, 49, 52, 55, 56, 60, 71, 72, 83, 88, 90, 92, 121, 129, 159, 161, 191, 203
business goals, 3, 31, 35, 37, 38, 39, 40, 41, 42, 45, 46, 49, 52, 53, 60, 63, 64, 65, 67, 68, 71, 72, 73, 98, 99, 101, 113, 120, 121, 129, 159, 161, 193, 195, 203

business process reengineering, 4
business processes, 5, 15, 16, 18, 56, 167, 176
business-IT relation, 13, 17, 20, 130
cascading architectures, 146
chain of justification. see justification
classification, 47, 48
CobiT, 131
completeness, 6, 25, 71, 116, 120
complexity, 12
COSO, 131
cost, 51
cultural, 123, 136, 147
culture, 91
definitions
    business driver, 36
    business goal, 38
    model, 101
    principle, 64
    requirement, 111
    stakeholder, 46
    standard, 106
design
    design process, 63, 64, 122, 210
    design vs. architecture, 6, 7, 148
    design work, 7, 27, 110, 147, 150

Index

designer, 8, 113

Digital Equipment Cooperation, 3

DNA, 49, 135

engineering, 7

enterprise architecture, 18, 19, 63

essential, 4, 6, 12, 13, 15, 16, 20, 24, 41, 50, 54, 60, 61, 64, 87, 88, 89, 92, 95, 98, 100, 110, 114

eTOM, 14, 147

fit-for-purpose, 8, 13, 19, 24, 25, 148

goal-means hierarchy, 68, 70, 71, 113

goodness, 6

governance
    architecture governance, 120, 128, 131
    IT governance, 120, 130, 131

heuristic, 7, 14, 15, 23, 24, 50, 54, 55, 95, 109, 122, 137, 148, 151

IEEE-1471, 3, 13, 24

implications, 64, 67, 68, 71, 84

information, 15

infrastructure, 12, 16, 17, 18, 23, 24, 52, 53, 131, 136, 150, 153

innovation, 14, 16, 23, 112, 147, 161

ISO, 4

ITAC, 151, 152

ITIL, 56, 57, 131

ITSA framework, 30, 32, 49, 59, 64, 67, 73, 101, 105, 106, 107, 113, 119, 120, 121, 138, 179

justification, 26, 49, 54, 64, 67, 119, 193, 195

KPI, 167, 169, 170, 191

litmus test, 83

metrics, 31, 32, 40, 41, 174, 177, 191, 203

Microsoft Certified Architect program, 151, 152

motional energy, 26

newness, 12

obstacles, 64, 68, 84

Open Group, 4, 15, 19, 151, 152, 211

organization type, 55

outsourcing, 36, 40, 55, 56, 57, 88, 173, 208

paper consuming, 26

people, process, technology, 61, 68, 84, 87, 90

policies, 74, 83, 175, 177

political, 40, 66, 123, 139, 147

PRINCE II, 107, 122

principles, 7, 60, 61
    composite principles, 80
    guidance, 82
    implications, 67, 84
    linking, 83
    litmus test, 83
    obstacles, 68, 84
    orthogonality, 80
    power, 63
    range and reach, 61

Index

rationale, 66
statement, 65
superfluous principles, 81
PRISM, 2, 4, 201, 209
procedures, 107
project hand over, 121
project requirements, 112
quality of service, 51
rationale, 64, 66, 83
realization project, 27, 68, 84, 102, 105, 113, 120, 135
reference architecture, 60, 78, 92, 133, 209
regulatory, 36, 56, 68, 191
request for proposal (RFP), 33, 119
requirements, 7
   architectural, 110
   engineering, 117
   project requirements, 112
   requirement vs. principle, 114
   requirements-gathering, 116
resistance, 26
reuse, 132, 133

RightStep™, 33
risk, 51, 78
risk-mitigating, 84
Sarbanes-Oxley, 36, 68
sense making, 12, 24, 91, 138, 146, 147
separation of concerns, 1, 2, 3, 4, 8, 17, 45, 49, 50, 146
services organization, 56
social, 17, 24, 61, 150
solution architecture, 3, 17, 18, 60, 132, 209
solutions, 17
stakeholder, 2, 11, 13, 46, 50
stakeholder analysis, 47, 51
SWOT, 42, 159, 161, 162, 190, 191
system thinking, 5
taxonomies, 89
TOGAF, 33, 129, 151, 209
tool, 71, 72
Vitruvius, 144, 149
V-lifecycle, 111
Zachman, 3, 33, 156, 157